Egg

Egg

from benedict to brûlée

MURDOCH
BOOKS

contents

the good egg

For as long as there has been appreciation of good food, there have been hens laying eggs for human use and consumption.

Cultures and religions have long held the egg as a symbol of life, regeneration and fertility. Early Sanskrit manuscripts tell of a cosmic egg containing a spirit that would be born, die and be reborn, while Christians use the egg as a symbol of rebirth in their Easter celebrations. Areas as diverse as the decorative arts, architecture and even nursery rhymes (think Humpty Dumpty) have all been inspired by the simplicity and perfection of the egg's design.

Today, this fascination is just as strong: immunologists, for example, are investigating whether the hen's ability to pass antibodies on to its egg can be useful to humans, such as in the treatment of snake bites or the prevention of tooth decay.

For many of us, of course, the appeal of eggs lies elsewhere—namely, in the kitchen. There is something very hands-on about cooking with eggs—from the first crack of shell against bowl to the triumphal carrying of soufflé to the table—that is immensely satisfying. Perhaps it is because eggs are used in such a variety of ways: sweet and savoury; simple or elaborate; healthy to downright decadent. And, though we may not be immunologists, it's worth knowing how eggs work, if for no other reason than to ensure a perfect poached egg in the morning.

selecting the best

While not many of us know the farmer behind the eggs we buy, let alone the hen, ensuring quality and freshness is not hard. There is an ever-increasing range on offer, driven by consumers' demands for eggs that have been laid by hens in healthy and humane conditions.

Hen eggs These are the eggs we are all familiar with. One popular misconception is that brown hen eggs are somehow more nutritious or flavoursome than white hen eggs, but this is not the case. Shell colour merely reflects the breed of the laying bird.

Quail eggs These miniature-sized, prettily speckled eggs have a more delicate flavour than hen eggs, and are popular for pickling, canapés and garnishing. Very fresh quail eggs can be used for poaching and ones that are a few days old are suitable for hard-boiling.

Duck eggs Larger and stronger in flavour than hen eggs, duck eggs are extremely rich, with quite gelatinous whites. Although they are sometimes cooked on their own, such as in omelettes, their richness means that they are best used in custards, pasta dishes and cakes. Duck eggs are unsuitable for making soufflés or meringues because of insufficient globulin, necessary in egg whites to trap and hold air when whisked. Duck eggs have a pretty pale blue or white shell.

what's in a name
The following is a brief guide to the multi-branded world of egg production. Note that eggs from commercial farms are infertile.

Cage-laid These form the greatest number of any type of commercially-produced egg, due to the intensive method of production. They are also often the cheapest. There are opponents to this system of production, however, who argue that the savings won are at the expense of the hen.

Barn-laid Also known as cage-free. Eggs laid by hens that are enclosed but have floor space covered in straw or similar materials.

Free-range Eggs laid by hens that have continuous access to nesting boxes, open floor space, perches and outdoor runs that contain vegetation.

Organic These eggs are produced in the same way as free-range eggs but their environment, including the land on which their food was grown, has been certified as free from herbicides and pesticides.

Designer Research has shown that varying the diet of the hen can affect the nutritional content of its egg. Designer or 'smart' eggs include the omega-3 eggs, which contain higher amounts of beneficial omega-3 fatty acids, as well as Vitamin E. Vegetarian eggs are laid from hens whose diet is free of meat and fish. Usually, such eggs are from caged birds as their diet is easily controlled. Future 'designer' eggs may include ones with lower cholesterol levels or greater mineral content.

nutrition
For a reliable, easy source of high quality protein it's hard to ignore the egg. In fact, the essential amino acids found in eggs are second only to those found in mother's milk. Eggs contain varying amounts of vitamins A, D, E and each one of the B complex vitamins, including B12. About the only thing missing is Vitamin C. Eggs are also an excellent source of iron and other minerals, such as potassium, phosphorus and zinc. Eggs contain no carbohydrates and about 59 calories (248 kj).

Cholesterol Eggs and cholesterol have a bad name but recent research indicates that the egg is not the culprit once thought. It is the level of saturated fat in the diet, rather than cholesterol, that has most impact on blood cholesterol levels. And, while eggs do indeed contain fat, more than half of the fat is of the 'good' mono- and polyunsaturated sorts. In terms of cholesterol, eggs contain 225 mg, all of which is found in the yolk.

when buying

Only buy eggs whose shells are clean, dry, of good colour and without any visible cracks. Eggs quickly lose their freshness at room temperature, so buy eggs that are in their carton and, ideally, stored in a refrigerator.

Grades This is not an indication of freshness or size but of quality of egg formation. Generally, only the two top grades AA and A are seen in supermarkets.

Carton dates Eggs are sold with a use by date, which corresponds to between 21 and 30 days after laying. Some cartons also have a packing date stamped on it.

Egg size and weight The size of an egg is influenced by several factors, the major one being the age of the hen. The older the hen, the bigger the egg. Sizes are classified by weight per dozen eggs and range from jumbo, extra-large, large, medium and small. Brown eggs are usually larger (and therefore more expensive) than white eggs.

storing fresh eggs

It's hard to imagine what life must have been like for the cook before the refrigerator. In the past, in order to maintain freshness, eggs have been immersed in mixtures of salt and wet clay, dry packed in wood ashes, or the shell coated with cactus juice. Nowadays, it's all too easy. Storing eggs in their carton in the refrigerator will keep them fresh for up to 3 weeks. The carton will also help prevent the eggs from absorbing the smells and flavours of other foods in the refrigerator. If refrigeration is not possible, coat the eggs in oil and keep them in a cool place.

Remember to take eggs out of the refrigerator 30 minutes before cooking, as they are best used at room temperature.

composition

An egg takes from 20 to 24 hours to form, beginning with the yolk and working outwards.

Egg shell Brittle and porous, the shell is the first line of defence for the egg. It is made mainly of calcium carbonate and its thickness and strength are largely determined by the hen's diet. Countless tiny pores cover the shell, allowing for the passage of water and gases. When fresh, a thin, transparent bloom covers the pores, thus preventing bacteria from entering the egg. As the egg ages, however, this bloom breaks down and there is greater contact with the outside world, leading to a subsequent loss of freshness.

Shell membrane Inner and outer membranes completely enclose the yolk and egg white, protecting them from bacteria. The outer membrane is connected to the eggshell.

Air cell As a newly laid egg cools, the contents shrink slightly, creating a pocket of air between the membranes at the shell's wider end. Over time, this air cell increases.

Egg white Also called egg albumen. None of the fat and more than half the egg's protein is found here. A very fresh egg may have a cloudy egg white, due to carbon dioxide. In older eggs, the gas has had time to escape through the shell.

Chalaza These are ropey strands of white that anchor the yolk in the centre, and are another indication of freshness. Some cooks strain them out of custards and sauces.

Yolk The yellow part of the egg makes up about 33% of an egg's liquid weight. The yolk contains all the fat, slightly less than half of the protein, and all of the egg's store of vitamins A, D and E, as well as many minerals. Colour is largely determined by the diet of the hen, which can also alter the flavour of the yolk. A diet supplemented with omega-3 can add a slightly fishy flavour to the eggs.

how egg proteins work

Understanding how an egg works can go a long way to ensuring the success of a recipe. By managing the temperature and rate of cooking, the actions of the proteins can be controlled.

Coagulation Egg proteins come coiled in a triangular shape. When the egg is heated, the proteins uncurl, thicken and form new bonds, often trapping liquid particles or air bubbles in the process. The temperature and speed at which the proteins 'set', or coagulate, will greatly determine the success of a recipe. Coagulation can also be affected by the addition of other ingredients. Salt and acids such as lemon juice actually encourage coagulation, while cream, sugar or alcohol slow it, by raising the temperature at which eggs coagulate. Curdling results when the proteins are heated past their coagulation point, such as when making a custard, and the proteins form bonds with each other, squeezing out the liquid, rather than retaining it.

Foaming Egg whites are known as leavening agents because of their ability to trap and hold air when beaten. When egg white is whisked, its constituent parts (protein and water) are separated. The proteins uncurl themselves, exposing amino acids: some of these repel water, others attract. With the subsequent jostling that occurs, as the amino acids form new bonds, the air particles are trapped and the characteristic large volume of foam results. When heated, for example when cooking a soufflé, the air bubbles expand and the protein film on the foam coagulates, producing a light, porous texture. When egg whites are overbeaten, too many bonds form between the proteins and a lumpy, dry mixture results.

Emulsification This is the ability of proteins in egg yolk to bind with the particles of one liquid, such as oil, and evenly suspend them throughout another liquid, such as water. The proteins prevent the two liquids from separating, which they would normally do. This is the basis for sauces like mayonnaise.

Coating When eggs are used in frying they bind with the coating, such as breadcrumbs, and form a seal. In this way they prevent the fat from soaking into the food.

does age matter?

As an egg ages, the whites become thinner and the yolk flattens. This affects the egg's appearance, particularly important if frying or poaching an egg. Older eggs can be useful when hard-boiling eggs, as very fresh eggs can be difficult to peel. The optimum age for an egg that is to be hard-boiled is 1 week old; up to 2 weeks is fine. For baking cakes and quiches, use eggs up to 3 weeks old.

Testing for freshness To test raw eggs for freshness, put an egg in a glass of water. If fresh, it will sink, if not it will float. This is due to the air pocket that has developed inside.

food safety

Salmonella These bacteria cannot multiply below 4°C (40°F) and die at 71°C (160°F). So, keep eggs in the refrigerator until needed, use good food handling practices, and cook eggs properly. When making recipes that contain raw eggs follow the instructions. The elderly, the ill, the young and the pregnant should avoid such recipes altogether.

Storing leftover eggs Egg whites can be stored for up to 5 days in a covered container in the refrigerator. Yolks can be stored for 2 days if kept in a bowl with plastic wrap pressed onto the surface and refrigerated.

Freezing leftover eggs Place egg whites in containers in recipe quantities, cover, label and freeze. Egg yolks and whole eggs should be beaten slightly first, then 1 teaspoon of salt or 1 tablespoon of sugar added for every 6 yolks or eggs. Cover, label salty or sweet, and freeze. Once defrosted, use immediately.

11

the indispensable egg

For those new to the kitchen, eggs can be a lesson in basic science, as well as an introduction to good cooking. Eggs bind dry ingredients, thicken custards and emulsify sauces. As well, the whites can be whisked to 8 times their volume. If all this sounds like potential disaster, then this section is for you.

how to boil an egg

The simple satisfaction to be gained from producing a perfectly boiled egg is not to be scoffed at. It's not hard either; apart from ignoring the instruction in the name—eggs are simmered not boiled—just keep an eye on the clock.

soft-boiled eggs

Bring a small saucepan of water to the boil. Put the egg onto a spoon and gently lower it into the water. Adjust the heat so that the water is simmering, not boiling and jiggling the eggs overly in the pan.

Cook for 4 minutes and then use a spoon to scoop out the egg. Transfer to an egg-cup, slice the top off, and eat. The yolk will be soft and runny, and the white just set—ideal for dunking with toast soldiers.

For medium-boiled eggs, follow the above method but allow the eggs to cook for 5–6 minutes before removing them from the water. The yolk, though still soft, is almost cooked and the white is fully set.

hard-boiled eggs

Put the eggs in a saucepan, and cover with cold water. If you wish, make a hole with a needle in the flatter end of the egg before putting it in the water. This allows the air to escape from the egg, thus avoiding any possibility of the shell cracking as the air expands with heating. This is not strictly necessary—use too heavy a hand with the needle and the shell may crack anyway.

Bring to the boil, then reduce and simmer for 8 minutes. Remove the eggs from the water, slice the top off and eat. The yolk should be fully cooked, and only slightly soft in the centre. The white will be fully cooked. If the egg is for later use, cool it under cold water to stop further cooking.

poaching eggs

The perfect poached egg is a much sought after creature, and suggestions abound as to how to ensure success. Whichever method you favour, it is essential that only really fresh eggs are used. Otherwise, little other intervention is needed.

Bring about 5 cm (2 in) water to the boil, or use boiling water from the kettle added to the pan, then reduce the temperature to the lowest simmering point possible.

Break the egg into a small bowl or saucer and, once the water is still, very gently slide the egg into the water. The egg can be broken directly into the water, but using a bowl or saucer gives greater control. Do not crack the eggs until they are needed.

Cook the egg for about 3–4 minutes, until the white has set and the yolk is just set on the surface and soft inside. Lift the egg out with a slotted spoon and drain on paper towel. Cut away any trailing bits of egg white, if you wish.

If poaching quail eggs, break the egg into a large spoon rather than a bowl. Rest the spoon just under the water for no more than 30–40 seconds, then remove; the egg should be cooked in this time.

boiled egg essentials

- Always use eggs that are at room temperature. The shells of eggs taken straight from the refrigerator may crack when added to the simmering water.

- Choose a saucepan just big enough to hold the eggs in a single layer. If too big, the eggs will be able to move around too much and possibly crack.

- Put the egg onto a spoon and gently lower it into the water. Reduce the heat so that the water is just barely boiling. This will prevent the egg from banging against the side of the pan and breaking its shell.

- Use a timer. A few extra minutes of cooking will mean the difference between soft, medium, hard-boiled or overcooked. If a hard-boiled egg has been overcooked there will be a grey ring around the yolk, and the texture will be quite rubbery. To prevent further cooking once the egg is out of the water, quickly cool it under cold running water before peeling.

poaching essentials

- For nicely rounded, good-looking poached eggs, the very freshest eggs must be used. Otherwise, the egg white will spread out around the yolk in all directions.

- Adding vinegar or lemon juice to the boiling water will help set the egg white but will also flavour the egg. If using, add only 1 teaspoon of either to the water.

- When and how the eggs should be added to the water is a matter of much debate. Some recipes recommend swirling the water to create a whirlpool before carefully adding the egg. Others recommend waiting until all of the tiny bubbles on the base of the pan have disappeared before adding. One quick option is not to wait at all, but remove the pan from the heat once the water comes to the boil, add the egg, cover, and leave it undisturbed for about 3 minutes until set.

poaching eggs

frying eggs

Most people feel confident about frying an egg. However, there is a big difference between a well-fried egg and the rubbery, truck-stop variety.

Bring the eggs to room temperature. Heat a heavy-based non-stick frying pan and add some oil and a knob of butter. When the butter is sizzling, carefully break the eggs into the frying pan and gently fry over a moderate heat, swirling the pan occasionally.

For eggs 'sunny side up', cook for about 1 minute, until the whites are set. As they cook, spoon some hot oil over the yolks so that the surface sets. Turn off the heat and leave to stand for 1 minute.

For eggs 'over easy', cook for 1 minute, until the whites are set, then use a spatula to turn the eggs over. Cook briefly for 30 seconds (no more) over low heat. For fully hard yolks, cook for 1 minute.

Carefully lift out the eggs with a metal spatula, place on paper towels to absorb any excess fat, then transfer to a plate. Season with salt and freshly ground black pepper, and eat immediately.

essentials

• Use only the very freshest eggs for frying, as both white and yolk will hold their shape better if fresh.

• The trick to frying eggs is to strike the right balance of heat—that is, high enough that the egg sets before spreading out too much but low enough so that the underside doesn't burn before the yolk is cooked.

• For best results, wait until the butter sizzles in the pan but is not yet browning, then add the egg to the pan. Adding a little oil to the butter will prevent the butter from burning so easily.

scrambling eggs

The wonder of scrambled eggs is that they can keep everyone happy, from purist to hedonist. As with all egg cooking, a gentle hand will achieve best results.

Break 2 large eggs into a clean, dry bowl and beat lightly with a fork to break up. Add 2 tablespoons of milk and season with salt and pepper. Mix together with a fork—depending on your preference, mix thoroughly for an even yellow colour, or just stir through for a streaky consistency.

Put a knob of butter (about 10 g/^{1}/4 oz) in a heavy-based non-stick saucepan and melt over a medium heat. Swirl to coat the pan with the butter, making sure it doesn't burn or turn brown.

Add the eggs and cook for 30 seconds. Using a flat-ended wooden spoon, slowly but constantly fold the mixture around as it cooks. Cook for about 1 minute, lifting and folding, until it is softly scrambled.

Remove the pan from the heat while there is still a little liquid left in the base—the eggs will cook for a little longer—add black pepper and serve immediately.

essentials

- The amount of milk or cream added to eggs to make a creamier, softly scrambled dish is very important. If too much liquid is added, then the proteins in the eggs become fully saturated upon even the slightest overheating and will squeeze the liquid out, forming a mass of solids in a pool of liquid. The recommended amount is 2–4 teaspoons of liquid per egg.

- Sometimes scrambled eggs may develop a greenish hue and although not attractive, the colour change is harmless. This usually occurs when the eggs have been cooked at too high a temperature, cooked for too long, or cooked in aluminium.

making the perfect omelette

The omelette is a classic example of the egg's versatility, as it can be adapted to suit an amazing variety of ingredients, techniques and appearances. For a simple, nutritious and really tasty meal, however, not much beats the simple folded omelette.

Break 3 eggs into a clean bowl and season well with salt and black pepper. Put a large knob (about 15 g/1/2 oz) of butter in an omelette or small frying pan and heat until foaming. Meanwhile, lightly beat the eggs with a fork to aerate slightly.

When the butter is ready, immediately add the eggs and cook for about 20 seconds, allowing the eggs to set slightly on the base, before stirring the egg mixture with a fork. Work quickly, drawing away some of the cooked egg from the bottom and letting some of the liquid egg set, tilting the pan a little as you work. If making an omelette with a filling, now is the time to add it to the middle of the just set eggs.

When most of the egg is set and the underside is golden, slide a small palette knife under the cooked egg to loosen it a little. Fold one-third of the omelette over the centre, then fold the remaining third over the top of the first. This will encase the filling if you have added one. The omelette should still be soft on the inside and a golden colour on the outside. Cook for 1 minute more, if necessary.

When ready, slide the omelette from the pan onto a serving plate and let it sit for 1 minute before serving.

eggs en cocotte

These quick and tasty little French baked eggs are real comfort food, not least because they are almost impossible to mess up. They are also a great way to use up whatever leftovers you may have, such as ham, mushrooms, cheese and capsicum (pepper).

Preheat the oven to 180°C (350°F/Gas 4). Lightly grease a 125 ml (1/2 cup) ramekin or ovenproof dish. Gently break an egg into the dish and spoon over 1 tablespoon thick (double/heavy) cream. Season with a little salt and freshly ground black pepper.

Place the ramekin into a roasting tin and fill the tin with enough boiling water that it comes half way up the outside of the ramekin. If making more than one at a time, make sure that the little dishes do not touch each other.

Place in the preheated oven and cook for 12 minutes. Remember that due to the heat retained by the ceramic dish, the yolks will continue to cook a little even after they have been removed from the oven. Sprinkle the eggs with chopped fresh herbs such as chives, tarragon and basil. Serve immediately, accompanied with slices of buttered toast.

omelette essentials

- This is one instance where the right equipment will make a difference. If you haven't got an omelette pan, however, use a good heavy-based, non-stick frying pan. Also, don't use a pan larger than need be; a pan 15–20 cm (6–8 in) in diameter is sufficient for a two- or three-egg omelette.

- Add a little oil to the butter in the frying pan, as this will help prevent the butter from burning too easily.

- When you add the beaten egg, and as you are cooking it, tilt the pan to distribute the egg evenly. Work quickly—the finished omelette should be golden on the outside but still soft and almost custard-like on the inside. Speed is the key to success here.

- As an alternative to folding the omelette in thirds, when the top is still moist, add any fillings to one half, then fold the other half over. Cook gently for 1–2 minutes, then slide the omelette out of the pan and serve. Omelettes are traditionally folded in three, but this is just as good, and easier.

- Apart from folding, omelettes can also be rolled or left flat, cooked on one side or both. A soufflé-type omelette involves beating the egg whites separately before folding them into the yolk. This gives the omelette a fluffier texture.

eggs en cocotte variations

Any number of ingredients can be added to baked eggs. Add the following to the basic egg and cream recipe, omitting the herbs if preferred. For each dish:
- Sprinkle 2 tablespoons finely grated Cheddar cheese or Parmesan on top of the cream, before baking.
- Fry 2 small, finely chopped mushrooms. Put into the base of the dish, then top with the egg and cream.
- Fry 1 heaped tablespoon finely diced red capsicum (pepper). Put into the base of the dish, spreading it evenly, then top with the egg and cream.

making the perfect omelette

separating eggs

This is not difficult to do, but as this is the starting point for a good many recipes, it is worth noting here a few key tips. It is possible to buy what is known as an egg separator, but that seems to be missing the point, really.

Have two small bowls, one for the yolk, and the other for the white. If separating many eggs, for example when making meringue, use three bowls. Separate each egg one by one into the two bowls, and only transfer the white into the third bowl if successfully separated. This way, if a little yolk gets into one of the egg whites, only that one will be affected, not the whole batch.

Crack the shell over the bowl for the whites. Gently pass the egg yolk backwards and forwards between the two shells, letting all the white slip out.

Alternatively, crack the shell and gently tip the egg into your hand. Open your fingers and let the white slide out between them, holding the yolk in your cupped hand. Make sure your hands are absolutely clean and free of any traces of grease or fats if using this method.

whisking egg whites

The simple act of incorporating air by whisking it into egg whites produces marvellous results: beautiful glossy white peaks, up to 8 times the original volume. Though a risky business—both too much and too little whisking are to be avoided—it is worth mastering the art, as whisked egg whites form the basis of many recipes, from soufflés to meringues.

Put the egg whites in a large, clean bowl and, using a balloon or hand-held electric whisk, use a circular movement, whisking the whites from the bottom of the bowl upwards. Until you are comfortable with whisking egg whites, it is wise to use a balloon whisk, rather than an electric one. Although it takes longer, there is less danger of overbeating the eggs, which can happen with an electric whisk in just a few seconds.

It is important to recognize the stages the whites will go through as they are whisked. Recipes for cakes and mousses may ask for soft but not dry peaks, while soufflés need stiffly beaten whites.

Once the whites start to form peaks, lift the whisk out occasionally to judge whether or not the egg whites have been whisked sufficiently. If you require soft peaks, stop whisking when the whites still droop slightly from the upturned whisk.

When stiff but not dry peaks are required, whisk until the egg whites hold their position if held upside down on the whisk.

When making meringue, whisk until soft peaks have formed, then whisk in the sugar in small quantities, making sure it is fully mixed in before more is added. When ready, the whites will be stiff, smooth and glossy.

separating essentials

- It is easier to separate eggs when cold, and always use fresh eggs. The older the egg, the weaker the membrane around the yolk, and thus the greater the chance of a little yolk getting into the egg white. Once separated, let the whites come to room temperature before whisking them.

- Try and give the egg one firm crack against its rim, rather than crushing it. This way, there will be less chance of small bits of shell falling into the bowl.

whisking essentials

- Egg whites should be at room temperature before whisking and only whisk them when you are ready to use them, not in advance.

- Whenever egg whites are being beaten to obtain maximum lightness or volume, they are always beaten alone. Any trace of yolk can reduce the white's potential to foam by as much as two-thirds. Once the whites have been beaten, however, the fats can be folded through without having any impact on the leavening qualities of the beaten egg whites. Soufflés and sponges are prime examples of this process.

- Plastic bowls should not be used for whisking as they retain traces of fat on their surfaces; as well, they tend to retain odours from foodstuffs previously held.

- Glass bowls, wiped with vinegar to remove any fatty traces, are ideal for whisking egg whites. However, many cooks swear by the stabilizing benefits of copper bowls, which are much like the effects of cream of tartar. Copper bowls are useful for soufflés.

- If adding cream of tartar, only a very small amount—a pinch—is needed.

- While underbeaten egg whites will not hold their shape, overbeaten whites will have the appearance of 'cracking' and be lumpy. If this happens, there is nothing else for it but to start again with a fresh batch of whites.

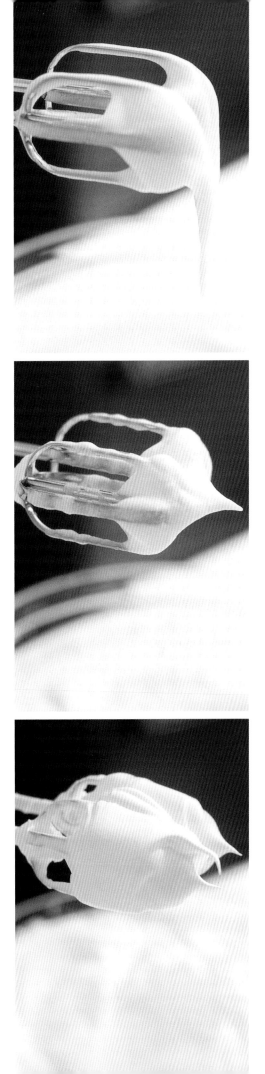

whisking egg whites

making egg-based sauces

Making your own mayonnaise or hollandaise may seem like an admirable but foolhardy endeavour, but it need not be so. Practice definitely does make a difference, and the satisfaction of serving your first luxuriously perfect eggs benedict is well worth the effort.

mayonnaise

4 egg yolks
1/2 teaspoon white wine vinegar
1 teaspoon lemon juice
1 teaspoon Dijon mustard (optional)
500 ml (2 cups) groundnut (peanut) oil

Makes about 500 ml (2 cups)

To make by hand, whisk the egg yolks, vinegar, lemon juice and mustard, if using, in a bowl until smooth. Then start adding the oil, drop by drop, whisking until the sauce stiffens slightly. When this occurs, add the oil in a thin, steady stream until all is combined. The key is not to rush it.

To make in a food processor, put the ingredients, apart from the oil, in a food processor and whisk or mix until creamy. With the motor running, slowly add the oil, a few drops at a time to begin with, and then as the emulsion forms, add in a thin, steady stream, until all is combined. Transfer to a bowl or jar.

When the mayonnaise is ready, season with salt and pepper, seal and refrigerate.

hollandaise sauce

180 g (6 oz) unsalted butter, cut into cubes
3 egg yolks
1 tablespoon lemon juice
2 teaspoons white wine vinegar

Serves 4

Begin by clarifying the butter. Put the butter in a small saucepan and bring to a simmer. Remove from the heat, skim off any scum on the surface, and let cool for a few minutes. Carefully pour the butter into a jug, leaving the sediment behind.

Half-fill a saucepan with water and bring to a simmer. Put the egg yolks, lemon juice, vinegar and 1 tablespoon water into a medium heatproof bowl and whisk until fully combined. Put the bowl over the water, making sure that it does not touch the water, and whisk for about 1 minute until the eggs are thick and foamy.

Slowly add the melted butter, whisking well until the sauce is thick and creamy. It should leave a trail if the whisk is lifted. Season well with salt and white pepper.

aïoli

4 egg yolks
4 garlic cloves, crushed
1/2 teaspoon salt
1–2 tablespoons lemon juice
500 ml (2 cups) vegetable or mild
   olive oil

Makes about 500 ml (2 cups)

To make the aïoli, put the egg yolks, garlic, salt and half the lemon juice in a food processor and mix until light and creamy. With the motor running, add the oil a few drops at a time until it begins to thicken, then add the remainder in a slow steady stream until fully combined.

Transfer to a bowl, add the remaining lemon juice to taste, season and thin with a little warm water, if necessary.

mayonnaise essentials

- Which oil you use will have a significant effect on the flavour of the mayonnaise. Canola oil, vegetable oil and light olive oil are good choices. The strong flavour of extra virgin oil can be too dominating.

- Make sure all the ingredients are at room temperature before starting.

- If the oil is added too quickly, it may cause the mayonnaise to 'break'. To rectify, rework the sauce into another egg yolk, adding the sauce gradually.

- If the mayonnaise becomes too stiff before all the oil is added, mix in a little more vinegar or lemon juice.

- Keep home-made mayonnaise in the refrigerator for up to 4 days only.

hollandaise essentials

- Clarifying the butter removes the milk solids and water in it, and gives a thicker sauce. Whole-butter hollandaise makes a thinner sauce, ideal for serving with fish.

- The key to this sauce lies in knowing when to stop whisking the egg yolks and water-based liquid in step 2—this first emulsion is known as a sabayon. The eggs need to be thickened enough to bind with the butter, but if kept on the heat for too long, or if the heat is too high, the eggs will cook and scramble. As the egg is whisked, it will increase in volume. When it stiffens slightly, immediately start adding the butter.

- Mousseline sauce is hollandaise made thick with whipped cream. Add 60 ml (2 fl oz) to the basic quantity. Serve with crab, poached fish and asparagus.

- For a foamier sauce, add egg whites, whisked to soft peaks, to the finished sauce. This is useful if making the sauce in advance, as the whites help prevent the sauce from curdling upon reheating.

hollandaise sauce

classic custards

Where would we be without custard-filled tarts, thick warm pouring custard or baked custard desserts such as crème brûlée or crème caramel? The custard is an essential. Once you have mastered these techniques, you can cook it with confidence.

crème anglaise

500 ml (2 cups) milk
1 vanilla pod, split in half lengthways
5 egg yolks
115 g (^{1}/2 cup) caster (superfine) sugar

Makes 750 ml (3 cups)

Pour the milk into a small saucepan and scrape the seeds from the vanilla pod into the milk, adding the pod as well. Whisk vigorously over medium heat to disperse the seeds and bring the milk to just below boiling point. Remove from the heat and allow to infuse for 10 minutes.

Whisk the egg yolks and sugar in a heatproof bowl for 3–4 minutes, or until thick and pale. Slowly add the milk, whisking constantly until all the milk has been added.

Clean the saucepan and pour the custard back into it. Cook over low heat, stirring constantly but gently with a wooden spoon until the custard is thick enough to coat the back of the wooden spoon. (To test for doneness, run your finger across the back of the wooden spoon. If the line holds its shape, then it is ready.) Pour the custard into a clean bowl and place over iced water to prevent any further cooking. Stir occasionally until cool.

Strain the custard through a fine strainer into a bowl or jug and serve. If not using it immediately, strain into a clean bowl and lay plastic wrap directly on the surface to prevent it from forming a skin. Refrigerate for up to 2 days.

simple baked custard

4 eggs plus 2 egg yolks
1 teaspoon pure vanilla extract
300 ml (10^1/2 fl oz) cream
200 ml (7 fl oz) milk
70 g (scant ^{1}/3 cup) caster
  (superfine) sugar
butter, for greasing
grated nutmeg

Serves 6

Preheat the oven to 150°C (300°F/Gas 2). Using a wooden spoon, lightly combine the eggs, yolks and vanilla. Do not whisk, as you do not want air incorporated.

Put the cream, milk and sugar in a saucepan and heat to just below boiling point. Pour slowly over the eggs and gently stir through.

Strain the mixture into a jug, then pour into six small (125 ml/^{1}/2 cup) buttered ramekins or one large (750 ml/3 cups) buttered ovenproof dish. Sprinkle over the grated nutmeg.

Carefully place the custard in a medium size roasting tin, then gently pour boiling water into the tin, until it comes about half-way up the outside of the dish.

Use oven gloves to place the tin in the oven, as it will now be very hot. Bake the custards for 20 minutes if in individual ramekins or for 30 minutes if in a large dish. The custard is ready when it is just set but still has a slight wobble. Remove from the water bath to prevent further cooking. Serve warm or slightly chilled.

custard essentials

- Though custards come in many guises the basic elements remain remarkably simple and consistent: yolks and/or whole eggs, cream or milk, sugar, salt and other flavourings. Eggs act as the thickener and the egg yolks, in particular, make custards smooth and rich. The differing results are achieved through varying the proportions of ingredients used and the method of preparation—that is, whether the custard is prepared by stirring on the stovetop or baked in the oven.

- Slow cooking or baking and gentle heat are vital if the speed at which the egg proteins coagulate is to be controlled. This is essential for a smooth, silky custard.

- When custards are overcooked, the egg proteins separate from the liquid in the mixture. In stirred mixtures this is known as curdling, and as weeping in baked custards. If curdling has not progressed too far, remove the mixture from the heat and stir or beat vigorously for a few minutes—this may reverse the process. In some recipes, starch (flour, cornflour and/or arrowroot) is added. Even very small amounts of starch will prevent the egg proteins from forming bonds too quickly, and thus greatly reduce the possibility of it curdling.

stirred custard essentials

- When making a stirred custard, take care not to allow the custard to come to the boil once you have returned it to the stove. Stir the mixture constantly to prevent the bottom from curdling.

- Have a bowl of iced water ready before you begin cooking. If the custard starts to overcook a little, arrest the process at once by sitting it in the bowl.

- To prevent a skin forming on top of cooling custards, press a layer of plastic wrap on the surface when the custard is still warm.

crème anglaise

the breakfast egg

Starting the weekend with eggs is, for some, the only way to start. Eggs are the classic breakfast ingredient, and can be fried, scrambled, poached or boiled to suit everyone's taste. It needn't stop there, however, as the following recipes show. Try French toast with crispy prosciutto, moreish little savoury tarts or rich blueberry pancakes.

eggs benedict

The key to great eggs benedict is getting the hollandaise sauce just right. It should be wonderfully smooth and rich. The following method uses a food processor, which is quicker than the traditional hand-whisked version, but you need to keep a close eye on it, as it can quickly curdle. This is one activity where multi-tasking is not recommended.

hollandaise sauce
175 g (6 oz) butter
4 egg yolks
2 tablespoons water
1 teaspoon tarragon vinegar

8 very fresh eggs
4 thick slices rye bread or
   4 English muffins
8 slices of leg ham

Serves 4

To make the hollandaise sauce, put the butter in a small saucepan and bring to a simmer. Skim off any scum that comes to the surface, then pour the butter into a jug, leaving the whitish sediment behind.

Put the yolks, water and tarragon vinegar in a small food processor or blender and, with the motor running, gradually pour in the melted butter. Whizz until the sauce is thick, creamy and buttery.

Put 5 cm (2 in) water in a deep saucepan and bring to the boil. Immediately reduce the heat to very low and wait until the water is still and there are only a few tiny bubbles on the base of the pan. Break the eggs, one by one, into a small bowl or saucer and then gently slide them into the water. Cook the eggs for about 3 minutes, or until the white has set. Cook the eggs in batches.

Meanwhile, toast the bread or muffins. Arrange on plates and top with the ham. Using a slotted spoon, remove the eggs from the pan and drain on paper towels. Cut away any trailing bits of egg white. Set the poached eggs on the ham, pour over the hollandaise sauce, add plenty of freshly ground black pepper and serve.

variations
Instead of ham, use wilted baby English spinach leaves, smoked salmon, steamed fresh asparagus, or thinly sliced and sautéed swiss brown mushrooms.

fried eggs and tomatoes on spring onion potato cakes

This delicious combination of eggs, potatoes and garlicky tomatoes is ideal for those days when you hanker for more than fried eggs on toast. The potato cakes take a little while to prepare, so make twice the amount and freeze half for use on another occasion.

2 tablespoons olive oil
1 garlic clove, sliced
3 Roma (plum) tomatoes,
  halved lengthways
2 tablespoons vegetable oil
4 very fresh eggs

spring onion potato cakes
300 g (10^1/2 oz) potatoes, peeled and
  roughly chopped
1 egg yolk
50 g (1^3/4 oz) grated Cheddar cheese
3 spring onions (scallions), trimmed and
  finely chopped
2 tablespoons finely chopped flat-leaf
  (Italian) parsley
1 tablespoon plain (all-purpose) flour
2 tablespoons olive oil

Serves 2

To make the spring onion potato cakes, boil the potatoes in a saucepan of salted water until tender. Drain well, then return the potatoes to the pan over low heat to evaporate off any remaining moisture. Remove the pan from the heat and mash the potatoes. Stir in the egg yolk, cheese, spring onions and parsley. Season well. Form into 4 small patty shapes. Tip the flour onto a plate and coat the patties with it. Cover and chill for 30 minutes.

Heat the olive oil in a large frying pan over medium heat. Fry the patties for 4–5 minutes on both sides until golden brown. Keep warm until needed.

Meanwhile, in a separate frying pan, cook the garlic and tomatoes. Heat the olive oil in the pan over low heat. Add the garlic and fry for 2 minutes. Add the tomatoes cut side down and fry for 10–15 minutes, turning them over once during cooking.

While the tomatoes are cooking, cook the eggs. Heat a heavy-based non-stick frying pan and add the vegetable oil. Break all 4 eggs, if possible, into the frying pan and fry over a moderate heat, swirling the pan occasionally.

Cook for about 1 minute, until the whites are set. As the eggs cook, spoon some hot oil over the yolks so that the surface sets. Turn off the heat and leave to stand for 1 minute. Serve the eggs on top of the spring onion potato cakes, accompanied by the tomatoes.

piperade

2 tablespoons olive oil
1 large onion, thinly sliced
2 red capsicums (peppers), seeded and
   cut into batons
2 garlic cloves, crushed
750 g (1 lb 10 oz) tomatoes
pinch of cayenne pepper
8 eggs, lightly beaten
1 tablespoon butter
4 thin slices of ham, such as Bayonne
buttered toast, to serve

Serves 4

Heat the oil in a large, heavy-based frying pan, then add the onions. Cook for about 3 minutes, or until soft. Add the capsicum and garlic, cover and cook for 8 minutes, stirring frequently to ensure the mixture doesn't brown.

Meanwhile, score a cross in the base of each tomato. Put in a large bowl of boiling water for 20 seconds, then drain and plunge into a bowl of cold water. Remove the tomatoes and peel the skin away from the cross. Chop the flesh and discard the cores. Add the chopped tomato and cayenne to the capsicum mixture, cover the pan and cook for a further 5 minutes.

Uncover the pan and increase the heat. Cook for 3 minutes, or until the juices have evaporated, shaking the pan often. Season well with salt and freshly ground black pepper. Add the eggs and scramble into the mixture until just cooked.

Heat the butter in a small frying pan and fry the ham. Place the buttered toast on 4 plates, arrange the piperade on top, lay the cooked ham alongside, and serve.

scrambled eggs and salmon on brioche

4 fresh eggs
4 tablespoons cream
2 tablespoons unsalted butter
125 g (4$^{1}/_{2}$ oz) smoked salmon, sliced
2 teaspoons finely chopped dill
2 small brioche or 2 croissants, warmed

Serves 2

Crack the eggs into a bowl, add the cream and beat together well. Season with some salt and freshly ground black pepper.

Melt the butter in a non-stick frying pan. When it starts to sizzle, add the eggs and turn the heat down to low. Using a flat-ended wooden spoon, push the mixture around until it starts to set, then add the salmon and dill. Continue to cook, gently folding the salmon and dill through the mixture until the eggs are mostly cooked, and just a little liquid is left in the pan.

Cut the top off the brioche or croissants, scoop out some of the filling, then pile the scrambled eggs on top, and serve.

mushroom omelette with chorizo

mushroom omelette with chorizo

50 g (1³/4 oz) butter
1 medium chorizo sausage, sliced
100 g (3¹/2 oz) mushrooms, sliced
6 eggs
2 tablespoons chives, finely chopped

Serves 2

Preheat the oven to 100°C (200°F/Gas ¹/2) and put in two plates to warm. Heat 30 g (1 oz) of the butter in a small omelette or frying pan over medium heat. Add the sliced chorizo and fry for about 5 minutes until golden. Remove from the pan using a slotted spoon. Add the sliced mushrooms to the pan and cook, stirring frequently, for about 4 minutes until soft. Add to the chorizo.

Break the eggs into a bowl and season well with salt and freshly ground black pepper. Add the chopped chives and beat lightly with a fork.

Put half the remaining butter in the pan and melt over medium heat until foaming. Add half the eggs and allow them to cook for 20 seconds, in which time they will start to set on the bottom, then quickly stir the mixture with a fork. Work quickly, drawing away some of the cooked egg from the bottom of the pan and allowing some of the uncooked egg to set, tilting the pan a little as you go. Once the eggs are mostly set, arrange half the sliced mushrooms and chorizo on top. Cook for 1 minute more, if necessary.

Carefully tip the omelette out onto a warmed plate and keep warm while you make the next one. Serve as soon as both omelettes are cooked.

mini savoury breakfast tarts

220 g (1³/4 cups) plain (all-purpose) flour
¹/2 teaspoon salt
140 g (5 oz) butter, chilled and diced
5 eggs
2 slices ham
1 tablespoon chopped parsley
1 medium tomato, thinly sliced
3 tablespoons cream
2 tablespoons grated Parmesan cheese

Serves 2

Preheat the oven to 200°C (400°F/Gas 6). Sift the flour and salt into a large bowl. Rub in the butter with your fingertips until the mixture resembles fine breadcrumbs. Add 1 egg and 2–3 teaspoons water and cut through with a palette knife to mix. Add a little extra water, if necessary.

Bring the dough together using your hands and shape into two balls. Wrap both balls in plastic wrap and refrigerate one for 10 minutes. Put the other ball in the freezer and use at another time.

Roll the pastry out on a floured work surface until it is very thin. Cut out two 16 cm (6¹/2 in) rounds and use them to line two 10 cm (4 in) tartlet tins. Press the pastry into the flutes of the tins. Don't worry if the pastry sticks up above the tin. Line each tin with a piece of baking paper and baking beads or some uncooked rice. Blind bake the pastry for 5 minutes, then remove the paper and beads or rice. Bake for 1 minute more.

Cover each pastry base with the ham (cut it into pieces to make it fit neatly). Add the parsley and tomato. Gently break 2 eggs into each tin, then pour half of the cream over the top of each. Sprinkle with Parmesan and add salt and pepper. Cook the tarts for 15 minutes, or until the egg whites are set. Serve hot or cold.

huevos rancheros with cheesy cornbread

Certain—let's say, unsophisticated—dishes seem to come and go from café menus without warning. For those of us who form attachments to the simple and hearty things in life there is only one solution: to champion them in the safety of one's own home.

1 tablespoon olive oil
1 small white onion, finely chopped
1/2 green capsicum (pepper),
    finely chopped
1 red chilli, finely chopped
1 garlic clove, crushed
1/2 teaspoon dried oregano
1 tomato, chopped
400 g (14 oz) tin chopped tomatoes
4 eggs
50 g (1/3 cup) feta cheese, crumbled

cheesy cornbread
155 g (11/4 cups) self-raising flour
1 tablespoon caster (superfine) sugar
2 teaspoons baking powder
1 teaspoon salt
110 g (3/4 cup) fine polenta (cornmeal)
60 g (1/2 cup) grated Cheddar cheese
25 g (1/2 cup) chopped mixed herbs, such
    as chives, dill and parsley
2 eggs
250 ml (1 cup) buttermilk
4 tablespoons macadamia or olive oil

Serves 2

Preheat the oven to 180°C (350°F/Gas 4). First make the cornbread. Sift the flour, sugar, baking powder and 1 teaspoon salt into a large mixing bowl. Add the polenta, cheese, herbs, eggs, buttermilk and oil and mix together. Spoon the mixture into a greased 18 x 8 cm (7 x 3 in) loaf tin and bake for 45 minutes, or until a skewer inserted in the centre comes out clean.

To make the huevos rancheros, put the olive oil in a large frying pan (one with a lid) and set over medium heat. Add the onion and green capsicum and gently fry for 2 minutes, or until soft.

Add the chilli and garlic and stir briefly, then add the oregano, fresh and tinned tomatoes and 90 ml (3 fl oz) water. Bring to the boil, then reduce the heat and gently simmer for 5 minutes until the sauce is thick. Season with salt and freshy ground black pepper.

Smooth the surface of the mixture, then make 4 hollows with a wooden spoon. Break an egg into each hollow and cover with the lid. Cook the eggs for 3 minutes, or until set.

When the bread is cooked, allow to cool in the tin before turning out. Serve the eggs with some feta crumbled over them and slices of the cornbread on the side, generously buttered.

croque-madame

3 eggs
1 tablespoon milk
1¹/2 tablespoons butter, softened
4 slices good-quality white bread
1 teaspoon Dijon mustard
4 slices Gruyère cheese
2 slices leg ham
2 teaspoons vegetable oil

Makes 2 sandwiches

Crack 1 egg into a wide, shallow bowl, add the milk and lightly beat. Season with salt and freshly ground black pepper.

Spread one-third of the butter over the bread, then spread half the slices with Dijon mustard. Place a slice of cheese on top, then the ham and then another slice of cheese. Top with the remaining bread.

Heat the remaining butter and vegetable oil in a large non-stick frying pan. While the butter is melting, dip one sandwich into the egg and milk mixture, coating the bread on both sides. When the butter is sizzling but not brown, add the sandwich and cook for 1¹/2 minutes on one side, pressing down firmly with a spatula. Turn over and cook the other side, then move it to the side of the pan.

Gently break an egg into the pan and fry until it is done to your liking. (For eggs 'sunny side up', cook for 1 minute until the whites are set. Spoon a little hot butter over the yolk so that the surface cooks.) Transfer the sandwich to a plate and top with the fried egg. Cover with foil and keep warm while you repeat with the remaining sandwich and egg, adding more butter and oil to the pan if necessary. Serve immediately.

french toast with crispy prosciutto

3 tablespoons thickened cream or milk
3 eggs
3 tablespoons caster (superfine) sugar
pinch of cinnamon
8 thick slices bread, cut in
  half diagonally
85 g (3 oz) butter
1 tablespoon olive oil
12 slices prosciutto

Serves 4

Put the cream, eggs, sugar and cinnamon in a wide, shallow bowl and mix together. Soak the bread in the egg mixture, one slice at a time, shaking off any excess.

Melt half the butter in a frying pan. When it is sizzling, add 3–4 pieces of bread in a single layer and cook until golden brown on both sides. Cook the remaining bread in batches, adding more butter as needed, and keeping the cooked slices warm in the oven until all are done.

Next, in a separate frying pan, heat the olive oil. When hot, add the prosciutto and fry until crisp. Remove and drain on paper towels. Place the prosciutto on top of the French toast and serve.

banana bread

3 ripe bananas, well mashed
2 eggs, well beaten
2 teaspoons grated orange zest
250 g (2 cups) plain (all-purpose) flour
1 teaspoon ground cinnamon
1 teaspoon salt
1 teaspoon bicarbonate of soda
180 g ($3/4$ cup) caster (superfine) sugar
70 g ($2^{1}/2$ oz) walnuts, coarsely chopped

Makes 1 loaf

Preheat the oven to 180°C (350°F/Gas 4). Grease a 17 x 8 cm (7 x 3 in) deep loaf tin.

Combine the bananas, eggs and orange zest in a large bowl. Sift over the flour, cinnamon, salt and bicarbonate of soda, mix, then add the sugar and walnuts. Mix thoroughly, then tip into the prepared tin. Bake for about 1 hour and 10 minutes, or until a skewer inserted into the centre comes out clean.

To serve, eat warm or allow to cool, then toast and serve buttered.

sweet toast with honey ice cream and fruit

Despite the addition of fresh nectarine, it will be difficult to convince anyone this is a dish for dieters. The toast should be sweet and slightly gooey, the ice cream rich and smooth.

25 ml (3/4 fl oz) cream
2 eggs
45 g (scant 1/4 cup) caster
   (superfine) sugar
60 g (21/4 oz) butter
6 slices bread (either fresh or day-old
   bread is suitable), cut in half diagonally
3 nectarines, cut into wedges

honey ice cream
375 ml (11/2 cups) milk
70 g (scant 1/3 cup) caster
   (superfine) sugar
1/2 vanilla bean, split
5 egg yolks
125 ml (1/2 cup) good-quality honey
250 ml (1 cup) whipping cream, chilled

Serves 4

To make the ice cream, put the milk and half the sugar in a saucepan. Scrape the seeds of the vanilla bean into the pan, adding the pod. Over medium heat, bring to just below boiling point, then remove from the heat and set aside for 10 minutes to infuse. Prepare a bowl of iced water. (This will be needed later for the custard.)

Put the egg yolks and remaining sugar in a bowl and whisk until light and creamy. Stop whisking when a ribbon of mixture leaves a trail across the surface.

Pour the infused milk in a thin stream onto the egg mixture, whisking steadily as the milk is added. Rinse the pan out, add the custard and return to the stove over very low heat. Using a wooden spoon, stir the mixture constantly for 8–10 minutes, or until it holds a clear shape when a line is drawn across the back of the spoon.

As soon as the custard is ready, transfer it to a bowl and place in the iced water. Stir in the honey. Allow the mixture to cool, stirring occasionally, then strain into a jug. Cover and refrigerate until cold. Stir the chilled cream into the custard base, pour into a freezerproof container and freeze for 3 hours until firm enough to scoop. Whisk with electric beaters for 2 minutes, then return to the freezer for 3 hours until solid. If using an ice cream machine, follow the manufacturer's instructions.

To make the sweet toast, mix together the cream, eggs and sugar in a bowl. Heat a little butter in a frying pan. Dip 2 triangles of bread into the egg, and shake off the excess. Cook on both sides until golden. Repeat with the remaining slices of bread, then serve with nectarine and ice cream.

ricotta flatcakes with honeycomb cream

150 g (1 cup) wholemeal flour
2 tablespoons caster (superfine) sugar
2 teaspoons baking powder
2 teaspoons ground ginger
55 g (1 cup) flaked coconut, toasted
4 eggs, separated
350 g (12 oz) ricotta cheese
310 ml ($1^1/4$ cups) milk
250 g (8 oz) mascarpone cheese
2 tablespoons icing (confectioners') sugar
75 g ($2^1/2$ oz) chocolate-coated
   honeycomb, coarsely crushed
4 bananas, sliced, to serve

Makes 18 flatcakes

Sift the flour, sugar, baking powder and ginger into a bowl. Stir in the coconut and make a dip in the centre. Add the egg yolks, ricotta and milk. Mix well to form a smooth batter. If too dry, add more milk.

In a separate bowl, beat the egg whites until soft peaks form, then fold them into the flatcake mixture to form a light batter.

Heat a frying pan and brush with a little melted butter or oil. Pour 3 tablespoons of the batter into the pan and gently swirl to create an even flatcake, about 10 cm (4 in) in diameter. Cook over low heat until bubbles form on the surface and it is golden on the underside. Turn over and cook the other side until golden. Keep the flatcakes warm while cooking the rest.

To make the honeycomb cream, put the mascarpone in a bowl, sift over the sugar and stir through. Just before serving, add the crushed honeycomb and stir until it is just combined but with chunks still visible.

To serve, stack the flatcakes on warmed plates. Top each stack with a generous dollop of the honeycomb mascarpone. Serve with some sliced banana.

blueberry pancakes

250 ml (1 cup) buttermilk
1 medium egg, lightly beaten
1 tablespoon melted butter
1 teaspoon pure vanilla extract
115 g ($3/4$ cup) plain (all-purpose) flour
1 teaspoon baking powder
$1/2$ teaspoon salt
2 ripe bananas, mashed
100 g ($3^1/2$ oz) blueberries
vegetable oil, for frying
maple syrup, to serve

Makes about 12 pancakes

Put the buttermilk, egg, butter and vanilla extract in a bowl and whisk together. Sift in the flour, baking powder and salt, and stir in. Don't overblend; the batter should be lumpy. Stir in the fruit.

Heat a little oil in a frying pan over medium heat. Pour 3 tablespoons of the batter into the pan per pancake. Cook for 3 minutes until the undersides are golden brown. Turn over and cook for 1 minute more. Repeat with the remaining batter, keeping the cooked pancakes warm. Serve immediately, drizzled with maple syrup.

raspberry breakfast crepes

Making crepes for breakfast is not a decision taken lightly, but these berry-filled crepes are not difficult to make, especially once the first, usually disastrous, crepe is out of the way. If that happens to you, just throw it away, thin the batter if necessary, and start afresh.

250 g (2 cups) plain (all-purpose) flour
pinch of salt
1 teaspoon sugar
2 eggs, lightly beaten
500 ml (2 cups) milk
1 tablespoon melted butter
400 g (14 oz) raspberries
icing (confectioners') sugar, for dusting
maple syrup or honey, to serve

Makes 8 large crepes

Sift the flour, salt and sugar into a bowl and make a well in the centre. In a jug or bowl, mix the eggs and milk together with 100 ml ($3^1/2$ fl oz) water. Slowly pour the mixture into the well, whisking all the time to incorporate the flour and ensure a smooth batter. Stir in the melted butter. Cover and refrigerate for 20 minutes.

Heat a crepe pan or a small non-stick frying pan and lightly grease. Pour in enough batter to coat the base of the pan in a thin, even layer. Tip out any excess. Cook over medium heat for 1 minute, or until the crepe starts to come away from the side of the pan. Do not be tempted to touch the crepe while it is cooking. Turn over and cook for 1 minute more until just golden. Repeat the process, stacking the crepes on a plate with pieces of grease-proof paper between them and covered with foil, until all the batter is used up.

To serve, put one crepe on a serving plate. Take one-eighth of the raspberries and arrange them on one-quarter of the crepe. Fold the crepe in half, then in half again, so that the raspberries are wrapped in a little triangular pocket. Repeat with the remaining crepes and raspberries. Dust with icing sugar, drizzle with maple syrup or honey, if you wish, and serve.

the portable egg

Normally, discovering your lunch crushed at the bottom of your bag would not be the ideal beginning to a picnic. However, with eggs, anything is possible. Pan bagnat actually improves with a little pressure, as this encourages the flavours to develop. For those who like things a little less rustic, there is much more on offer in this chapter.

quail eggs with spiced salts

2 teaspoons cumin seeds
48 quail eggs
120 g (1/2 cup) good-quality table salt
1 1/2 teaspoons Chinese five-spice powder
3 teaspoons celery salt

Makes 48

Toast the cumin seeds in a dry frying pan over low heat for 1–2 minutes, or until fragrant. Cool slightly, then grind in a spice grinder or small food processor, or use a mortar and pestle to finely crush into a powder.

Put half the eggs in a large saucepan of water, bring to the boil and cook for 1 1/2 minutes for medium-boiled eggs. Drain, then cool under cold running water and peel. Repeat with the remaining eggs.

Divide the salt among 3 small bowls and add the Chinese five-spice powder to one, the celery salt to another and the ground cumin to the third. Stir the flavourings into the salt in each bowl.

To serve, pile the eggs into a large bowl and serve with the small bowls of salt. Invite your guests to dip their egg into the flavoured salt of their choice.

thinking ahead
The eggs can be prepared the day before they are to be served and the spiced salts can be made up to 2 weeks ahead of time and stored in airtight containers.

chinese tea eggs

10 very fresh hen eggs
3 tablespoons light soy sauce
3 tablespoons Shaoxing rice wine
1 star anise
1 tablespoon light brown sugar
1 cinnamon stick
3 slices fresh ginger, smashed with the
    flat side of a cleaver
3 tablespoons Chinese black tea leaves

Makes 10 hen eggs

Put the eggs in a saucepan with enough cold water to cover. Bring to the boil, then reduce the heat to low and let the eggs simmer for about 10 minutes. Drain, then cool the eggs under cold running water. Lightly crack the shells but do not peel them. Set aside.

Put the remaining ingredients in a large pan filled with 1 litre (4 cups) water and bring to the boil. Reduce the heat slightly and simmer for about 20 minutes. Add the eggs and simmer for a further 45 minutes. Turn off the heat and let the eggs sit in the mixture until cool enough to handle, then peel, cut into wedges and serve.

super sauces with deep-fried squid

These classic sauces, when freshly made, add such a burst of flavour that they become almost more important than the dish they accompany.

extra special tartare sauce
200 g (7 oz) crème fraîche or sour cream
2 tablespoons mayonnaise
3 gherkins, finely chopped
2 tablespoons capers, finely chopped
1 teaspoon lemon juice
1 tablespoon chopped flat-leaf
  (Italian) parsley

Put all the ingredients in a serving bowl.
Mix well.

herb aïoli
4 egg yolks
4 garlic cloves, crushed
1 tablespoon chopped basil
4 tablespoons chopped flat-leaf
  (Italian) parsley
1 tablespoon lemon juice
200 ml (7 fl oz) olive oil

Put the egg yolks, garlic, basil, parsley and lemon juice in a small food processor and mix until light and creamy. With the motor running, add the oil, drop by drop, until the sauce begins to thicken. At this point, add the oil in a very thin stream until combined. Transfer the aïoli to a small serving bowl.

smoked garlic aïoli
250 ml (1 cup) mayonnaise
1 egg yolk
1 whole garlic bulb, unpeeled

Preheat the oven to 200°C (400°F/Gas 6). Wrap the garlic bulb in foil and bake for 30 minutes. Remove, unwrap and let cool, then squeeze the garlic out of each clove. Put the mayonnaise in a small bowl and whisk in the egg yolk. Use a pestle and mortar to mash the garlic until smooth, then add to the mayonnaise.

deep-fried squid
1 kg (2 lb 4 oz) baby squid, cleaned and
  tubes cut in half
250 ml (1 cup) milk
2 tablespoons lemon juice
3 tablespoons sea salt
3 tablespoons white peppercorns
1 teaspoon sugar
250 g (2 cups) cornflour
vegetable oil, for deep-frying
lime wedges, to serve

Serves 4 as a starter, with the sauces

Pat the squid tubes dry. Place them on a chopping board with the insides facing up, and cut a fine diamond pattern on the surface, taking care not to cut all the way through. Cut the tubes into rectangles and put them in a bowl. Cover with the milk and lemon juice and refrigerate for 15 minutes.

Put the salt, peppercorns and sugar in a mortar and pound with a pestle to a fine powder. Alternatively, use a spice grinder. Transfer to a bowl and stir in the cornflour. Toss the squid in the salt-and-pepper flour, thoroughly coating them.

To cook the squid, heat about 10 cm (4 in) oil in a small frying pan over medium heat until a cube of bread dropped in the oil turns brown in 15 seconds. Quickly deep-fry the squid in batches until crisp and lightly golden. Serve with lime wedges and one or all of the sauces.

caesar salad

1 cos (Romaine) lettuce
8 thin slices baguette
3 rindless bacon rashers, chopped
1 egg yolk
1 garlic clove
4 anchovy fillets
250 ml (1 cup) olive oil
1 tablespoon lemon juice
dash of Worcestershire sauce
1 lump of Parmesan cheese, to garnish

Serves 2

Tear the lettuce into pieces and put them
in a large bowl. Turn on the grill (broiler).

Brush the baguette slices on both sides
with a little oil and grill them until they are
golden brown all over. Set aside to cool.

Heat a little oil in a frying pan, add the
bacon and fry until crisp. Remove, pat dry,
then add to the lettuce.

Put the egg yolk, garlic and anchovies in
a food processor and whizz for a minute
or two. With the motor running, add the
remaining oil, a few drops at a time, then,
as the sauce thickens, increasing to a thin,
steady stream. When fully combined,
transfer to a bowl or jug, add the lemon
juice and Worcestershire sauce and mix
well. Season with salt and freshly ground
black pepper. Cover and refrigerate the
dressing until needed.

Using a potato peeler, make Parmesan
curls by firmly running the peeler along
one edge of the lump of cheese. Try to
make the curls as thin as possible.

Pour the dressing over the lettuce and
gently toss to mix. Divide the lettuce
between 2 bowls and arrange the slices of
toasted baguette and the Parmesan curls
on top of each one.

creamy egg salad

10 large eggs, plus 1 egg yolk
3 teaspoons lemon juice
2 teaspoons Dijon mustard
60 ml (1/4 cup) olive oil
80 ml (1/3 cup) safflower oil
2 tablespoons chopped dill
2 tablespoons crème frâiche or sour cream
2 tablespoons capers, rinsed and drained
20 g (1/3 cup) mustard or salad cress

Serves 4

Put the whole eggs in a pan of water. Bring
to the boil and simmer for 10 minutes.
Drain, then cool under cold water and peel.

To make the mayonnaise, put the egg yolk,
lemon juice and Dijon mustard in a food
processor and season. With the motor
running, slowly add both oils, drop by drop,
increasing to a thin, steady stream as the
mixture thickens. When combined, put the
mayonnaise in a large bowl, add the dill,
crème frâiche or sour cream and capers.

Chop the eggs and add to the mayonnaise.
Put in a serving bowl, sprinkle over just the
green tips of the mustard cress and serve.

salade lyonnaise

4 tablespoons olive oil
200 g (7 oz) piece speck, rind removed
  and cut into 1 cm (1/2 in) cubes
2 garlic cloves, thinly sliced
100 g (31/2 oz) crustless sourdough
  bread, cut into 1 cm (1/2 in) cubes
120 g (41/2 oz) frisee (curly endive)
  lettuce, washed and dried
80 g (1/4 cup) watercress, leaves only
4 very fresh eggs
2 tablespoons sherry vinegar
2 teaspoons chopped parsley

Serves 4 as a starter

Heat 1 tablespoon of the oil in a heavy-
based frying pan over medium heat. Add
the diced speck and sauté for 3–5 minutes
until golden. Add the garlic and cook for
about 2 minutes, or until soft but not yet
coloured. Remove the speck and garlic
with a slotted spoon, leaving as much of
the rendered fat in the pan as possible.
Set aside on paper towels.

Add the bread to the pan and fry until
golden, stirring frequently. Remove from
the pan and drain on paper towels.
Reserve the pan and its juices.

Divide the salad leaves among 4 plates,
sprinkle over the croutons, then spoon the
speck and garlic over the leaves and bread.

Put 5 cm (2 in) water in a wide frying pan,
bring to the boil, then reduce the heat to
very low. When the water is still, cook the
eggs in two batches. Crack the eggs one
at a time into a small bowl and add to the
water. Cook for 3 minutes, until set.
Repeat with the remaining two eggs.

Add the remaining oil to the reserved
frying pan, add the sherry vinegar and
parsley, and heat. Spoon the sherry
dressing over the leaves. Top with the
eggs, season to taste, and serve.

smoked salmon tortilla

Tortillas are ideal picnic food. They are usually generously filled with fresh ingredients; are cooked to a firmness just right for finger-food; and can be eaten warm or cold. This lovely summery recipe features smoked salmon, mascarpone and plenty of herbs.

1 tablespoon olive oil
200 g (7 oz) potatoes, peeled and cut
   into small cubes
1 small onion, finely chopped
4 eggs
2 tablespoons chopped flat-leaf
   (Italian) parsley
1 tablespoon dill, finely chopped
1 tablespoon chopped chives
4 slices smoked salmon (about 50 g/
   1 3/4 oz total weight) roughly chopped
   into small pieces
2 tablespoons mascarpone cheese
2 handfuls salad leaves, to serve

Serves 2

Heat the oil over low heat in a non-stick frying pan with a flameproof handle (a pan about 15–20 cm (6–8 in) in diameter is fine). Add the potato cubes and gently fry for about 10 minutes until cooked through to the middle and brown on all sides. Cut a cube open to see if they are cooked through completely.

When the potato is cooked, add the onion and gently cook for a few minutes until it is translucent. Turn on the grill (broiler).

When the onion is almost ready, break the eggs into a bowl and whisk them together with the parsley, dill and chives. Add salt and freshly ground black pepper.

Add the smoked salmon pieces to the frying pan, then the mascarpone in blobs. Using a wooden spatula, make sure the mixture is evenly distributed over the base of the pan and level it off. Pour the eggs over the top. Lightly swirl each blob of mascarpone with a spoon. Cook for 4 minutes, or until the tortilla is just set.

Put the frying pan under the hot grill for 1 minute to lightly brown the top of the tortilla. Gently slide the tortilla out of the frying pan and cut it into 4 slices. Arrange a handful of salad leaves on each plate and top with slices of tortilla. If taking on a picnic, leave to cool, then wrap in foil. Slice when ready to eat, and serve with salad leaves.

mini sweet potato and leek frittatas

1 kg (2 lb 4 oz) orange sweet potato
1 tablespoon olive oil
30 g (1 oz) butter
4 leeks, white part only, thinly sliced
2 garlic cloves, crushed
250 g (1 2/3 cups) feta cheese, crumbled
8 eggs
125 ml (1/2 cup) cream

Makes 12

Preheat the oven to 180°C (350°F/Gas 4). Grease twelve 125 ml (1/2 cup) muffin tin holes. Cut small rounds of baking paper and place into the base of each hole. Cut the sweet potato into small cubes and boil, steam or microwave until tender. Drain well and set aside.

Heat the oil and butter in a large frying pan, add the leek and cook for about 10 minutes, stirring occasionally until very soft and lightly golden. Add the garlic and cook for 1 minute more. Cool, then stir in the feta and sweet potato. Divide the mixture evenly among the muffin holes.

Whisk the eggs and cream together and season with salt and freshly ground black pepper. Pour the egg mixture into each hole until three-quarters filled, then press the vegetables down gently. Bake for 25–30 minutes, or until golden and set. Leave in the tins for 5 minutes, then ease out with a knife and cool on a wire rack before serving.

artichoke and red capsicum frittata

175 g (6 oz) broad beans, fresh or frozen
400 g (14 oz) tin artichoke hearts, drained well
3 tablespoons olive oil
1 onion, thinly sliced
1 small red capsicum (pepper), finely sliced
6 eggs
2 tablespoons chopped parsley
45 g (1/2 cup) pecorino cheese, grated
pinch of nutmeg

Serves 4

Bring a small saucepan of water to the boil and add a large pinch of salt along with the broad beans. Boil for 2 minutes, then drain and rinse the beans under cold running water. Peel away the skins.

Cut the artichoke hearts from bottom to top into fine 5 mm (1/5 in) thick slices. Discard any slices containing the tough central choke.

Heat the oil in a 30 cm (12 in) non-stick frying pan and add the onion and red capsicum. Fry over low heat for 7 minutes until the onion is soft but not brown. Add the artichoke slices and cook for a further 1–2 minutes. Add the broad beans and stir through to heat.

Preheat the grill (broiler). Put the eggs, parsley, pecorino and nutmeg in a bowl and lightly beat together. Season well with salt and freshly ground black pepper. Add to the frying pan, stirring to evenly distribute the ingredients. Cook over low heat for 8 minutes, or until three quarters set, shaking the pan often to stop the frittata sticking. Finish the top off under the grill and leave to cool before serving in wedges.

vegetable torte

150 g (5¹/₂ oz) asparagus
4 tablespoons olive oil
1 onion, chopped
1 zucchini (courgette), halved lengthways
　　and thinly sliced
2 garlic cloves, chopped
100 g (2¹/₂ cups) English spinach, stalks
　　removed if necessary, roughly chopped
2 tablespoons chopped basil
75 g (³/₄ cup) Parmesan cheese, grated
250 g (1 cup) ricotta cheese
250 g (1 cup) mascarpone cheese
6 eggs

Serves 6

Wash the asparagus, then remove and
discard the woody ends. Remove the spear
tips, reserve, and finely slice the remaining
stems. Bring a saucepan of salted water to
the boil and cook the asparagus stems for
about 2 minutes. Add the tips and cook
for 1 minute more. Drain the asparagus.

Preheat the oven to 180°C (350°F/Gas 4).
Heat the oil in a saucepan, add the onion
and cook until soft. Increase the heat and
add the zucchini. Cook until just turning
golden brown, stirring frequently. Add the
garlic and cook for 1 minute more, then
add the spinach and toss until wilted.

Remove the pan from the heat, add the
asparagus and basil, season with salt and
pepper and set aside to cool.

Grease a 20 cm (8 in) springform tin with
butter and dust with a tablespoon of the
Parmesan. Mix the ricotta, mascarpone,
eggs and 50 g (¹/₂ cup) Parmesan into the
cooled vegetables. Taste for seasoning.

Spoon the mixture into the tin and scatter
over the remaining Parmesan. Place on a
tray to catch any drips and bake for 50–60
minutes. After 30 minutes, cover with foil
to prevent over-browning. Cool for half an
hour, then chill for 3 hours before serving.

quiche with prosciutto and peas

For a dish with an image problem, the humble quiche remains ridiculously good, and is one of the stalwarts of egg cooking. It's also very versatile, as this version shows.

200 g (1³/4 cups) plain (all-purpose) flour
100 g (3¹/2 oz) unsalted butter, chilled
  and diced
4 tablespoons iced water
175 g (6 oz) prosciutto, roughly chopped
4 eggs
450 ml (16 fl oz) cream
65 g (2¹/3 oz) Cheddar cheese, grated
50 g (1³/4 oz) Gruyère cheese, grated
100 g (3¹/2 oz) frozen peas, defrosted
1 tablespoon finely chopped parsley

Serves 4–6

Preheat the oven to 180°C (350°F/Gas 4). Place a baking tray in the oven to preheat.

Put the flour, pinch of salt and butter in a food processor and mix, using the pulse button, until the mixture resembles fine breadcrumbs. Add the iced water a little at a time until the dough comes together.

Transfer the dough to a lightly floured work surface. Form it together with your hands into a ball, then flatten it. Wrap in plastic wrap and chill for 30 minutes.

Grease a fluted, loose-bottomed 24 x 3 cm (9¹/2 x 1 in) deep metal tart tin. Allow the pastry to come to room temperature, then roll out to a round just larger than the tin. Drape the pastry over the tin, then gently press it into the flutes. Cut off the excess pastry, then press the pastry up so that it just exceeds the rim of the tin, to allow for shrinkage. Chill for ¹/2 hour.

Line the pastry shell with baking paper and fill with baking beads or uncooked rice. Place on the preheated baking sheet and bake blind for 15 minutes. Remove the parchment and baking beads or rice and bake for a further 10 minutes until dry.

Meanwhile, heat a frying pan over high heat. Add the prosciutto and dry-fry until crisp. Break into pieces and set aside. Beat together the eggs and cream, and season. Place the prosciutto in the pastry case and sprinkle over the grated cheeses, peas and the parsley. Pour the eggs and cream mixture into the pastry case, taking care that it does not spill over the edges. Bake for 40 minutes, or until the pastry is cooked and the filling is set and golden. Allow to rest for 10 minutes before serving warm or at room temperature.

caramelized red onion and feta tartlets

These tartlets are actually quite crumbly little fellows. The simple pastry crust consists of nothing more than flour, butter and water, producing a short rather than pliable texture. Though they contain eggs and cream, they're not that rich—they're just yummy.

1¹/2 tablespoons olive oil
2 large red onions, finely chopped
2 teaspoons chopped thyme
70 g (scant ¹/2 cup) feta cheese, crumbled
2 eggs, lightly beaten
125 ml (¹/2 cup) cream

pastry
170 g (1¹/3 cups) plain (all-purpose) flour
75 g (2³/4 oz) butter
1–2 teaspoons iced water

Makes 24

Preheat the oven to 180°C (350°F/Gas 4). Heat the oil in a large frying pan (do not use the non-stick kind as the onion won't caramelize in that). Add the onion and cook, stirring occasionally, over low heat for 30 minutes, or until golden brown. Add the thyme, stir well and transfer the mixture to a bowl to cool.

To make the pastry, sift the flour and a pinch of salt into a large bowl. Add the butter and rub in with your fingers until the mixture resembles fine breadcrumbs. Add a little iced water and cut through the mixture with a knife until combined. Add more water if needed. Use your hands to form the pastry into a smooth ball. Wrap in plastic wrap and rest in the refrigerator for 30 minutes.

Grease twelve 125 ml (¹/2 cup) shallow patty tin holes. Allow the pastry to come to room temperature, then roll out to a large round. Using an 8 cm (3 in) cutter, cut out 12 rounds and line the holes.

Divide the onion among the patty cases, then spoon over the feta. Combine the eggs with the cream, season with salt and pepper, then carefully pour into the pastry cases. Bake for 10–15 minutes, or until puffed and golden. Leave the tartlets in the tins for 5 minutes before transferring to a wire rack to cool.

thinking ahead
These little feta tartlets can be made a day in advance and reheated in an oven preheated to 150°C (300°F/Gas 2). Heat for 10 minutes before serving.

classic egg sandwiches

A sandwich seems a fairly straightforward thing but appearances can be deceptive (as anyone who orders take-away sandwiches on a regular basis well knows). So, for the sake of office workers everywhere, here are three classic egg sandwich combinations.

egg and watercress
3 hard-boiled eggs, cooled and peeled
1 1/2 tablespoons mayonnaise
1 teaspoon softened butter
1 tablespoon finely chopped chives
10 g (1/3 cup) watercress, leaves only
4 slices wholegrain bread, buttered,
   crusts removed

Makes 2 sandwiches

Put the eggs, mayonnaise, butter and chives into a small bowl. Add salt and freshly ground black pepper, then mash together with a fork until evenly and well mixed but still slightly chunky. Wash and dry the picked watercress leaves.

Spread the egg mixture onto 2 slices of bread, top with the watercress and the remaining bread. Cut into quarters.

curried egg
3 hard-boiled eggs, cooled and peeled
1 1/2 tablespoons mayonnaise
2 teaspoons softened butter
2 teaspoons curry powder
4 slices rye bread, buttered,
   crusts removed

Makes 2 sandwiches

Put the eggs, mayonnaise, butter and curry powder into a bowl. Mash together with a fork until evenly mixed but still slightly chunky. Season well with salt and freshly ground black pepper.

Spread 2 slices of bread with the curried egg, top with the remaining slices, then cut in quarters and serve.

egg, olive and rocket
3 hard-boiled eggs, cooled and peeled
1 1/2 tablespoons mayonnaise
1 teaspoon softened butter
2 tablespoons finely shredded
   basil leaves
1 tablespoon chopped Kalamata olives
4 slices white bread, buttered,
   crusts removed
handful of baby rocket (arugula) leaves,
   washed and dried

Makes 2 sandwiches

Put the eggs, mayonnaise and butter into a small bowl. Mash together with a fork until evenly mixed but still slightly chunky, then add the basil leaves and olives. Stir well, then season to taste.

Spread the egg mixture onto 2 slices of bread, top with the rocket leaves, then the remaining slices of bread. Cut into quarters and serve

chargrilled steak baguette with rocket and mustardy mayo

3 tablespoons olive oil, plus extra for frying
1 red onion, sliced
1 teaspoon soft brown sugar
2 teaspoons balsamic vinegar
1 teaspoon fresh thyme, chopped
1 tablespoon Dijon mustard
3 tablespoons mayonnaise
100 g (3^1/$_2$ oz) rocket (arugula)
4 beef steaks (about 125 g/4^1/$_2$ oz
   each piece)
2 thick baguettes, cut in half, or 8 thick
   slices of good-quality bread
2 tomatoes, sliced

Serves 4

Heat 2 tablespoons olive oil in a frying pan.
Add the onion and cook very slowly, with
the lid on, stirring occasionally, until the
onion is soft but not brown. This could take
up to 15 minutes. Remove the lid, add the
sugar and vinegar and cook for a further
10 minutes until the onion is just browned
and soft. Take the pan off the stove and stir
in the thyme.

Meanwhile, make the mustardy mayo by
mixing together thoroughly the mustard
and mayonnaise in a small bowl.

Drizzle the rocket leaves with 1 tablespoon
olive oil and season with salt and freshly
ground black pepper.

Heat 1 tablespoon of the extra oil in a
frying pan over high heat and cook the
steaks for 2 minutes on each side, adding
more oil if necessary. Season to taste.

To serve, put out the bread, along with
separate bowls containing the onion,
mustardy mayo, rocket leaves, steak and
sliced tomatoes. Let everyone make their
own baguette so they can get their
preferred mix of all the flavours.

fried egg and red onion wrap

1 tablespoon olive oil
2 red onions, thickly sliced
1 red capsicum (pepper), sliced
1/2 tablespoon balsamic vinegar
2 eggs
2 lavash breads
2 tablespoons sour cream
sweet chilli sauce

Serves 2

Heat the olive oil in a non-stick frying pan and add the onion. Cook it slowly, stirring occasionally, until soft and translucent. Add the capsicum and continue cooking until both the onion and capsicum are soft. Turn the heat up and stir for a minute or two until they start to brown, then add the balsamic vinegar.

Push the mixture over to one side of the pan and carefully break both eggs into the other side, keeping them separate if you can. Fry over a gentle heat until the eggs are just set.

Briefly heat the lavash breads under the grill (broiler) or in a microwave to soften and warm them. Lay the breads out on a board, spread a tablespoon of sour cream over the centre of each, then drizzle over a little sweet chilli sauce. Pile the hot onion and capsicum mixture on each and top with an egg. Season with salt and freshly ground black pepper.

Fold in the short end of each piece of lavash bread, then roll up lengthways. Cut in half to serve, then eat immediately, with plenty of napkins nearby.

pan bagnat

4 crusty bread rolls
1 garlic clove
60 ml (1/4 cup) olive oil
1 tablespoon red wine vinegar
3 tablespoons basil leaves, roughly torn
2 tomatoes, sliced
2 hard-boiled eggs, sliced
75 g (2 1/2 oz) tin tuna
8 anchovy fillets
1 small cucumber, sliced
1/2 green capsicum (pepper), thinly sliced
1 French or baby shallot, thinly sliced

Serves 4

Slice the bread rolls in half and remove some of the soft centre from the tops. Cut the garlic clove in half and rub the insides of the rolls with the cut sides. Sprinkle both sides of the bread with the olive oil and vinegar. Season with salt and pepper.

Put all the sandwich ingredients on the base of the rolls, top with the other half and wrap each sandwich in foil. Press firmly with a light weight, such as a tin of food, and leave in a cool place for 1 hour before serving.

the evening egg

Dinner is the time when most of us attempt dishes that take us into uncharted culinary waters. Deep-fried zucchini flowers, potato gnocchi with pancetta and basil, and peppered beef with béarnaise sauce may seem the preserve of restaurants but they needn't be. Practice and good ingredients can achieve wonders.

crab and corn egg noodle broth

75 g (2 1/2 oz) dried thin egg noodles
1 tablespoon groundnut (peanut) oil
1 teaspoon finely chopped fresh ginger
3 spring onions (scallions), thinly sliced,
    white and green parts separated
1.25 litres (5 cups) chicken stock
80 ml (1/3 cup) mirin
250 g (9 oz) baby corn, sliced on the
    diagonal into 1 cm (1/2 in) slices
175 g (6 oz) fresh crab meat
1 tablespoon cornflour mixed with
    1 tablespoon water
2 eggs, lightly beaten
1 tablespoon soy sauce
2 teaspoons lime juice
7 g (1/4 cup) torn fresh coriander
    (cilantro) leaves

Serves 4

Cook the noodles in a saucepan of boiling salted water for 3 minutes, or until just tender. Drain and rinse under cold water.

Heat the oil in a heavy-based saucepan. Add the ginger and the spring onion (white part only) and cook over medium heat for 1–2 minutes. Add the stock, mirin and corn and bring to the boil. Simmer for about 5 minutes. Stir in the crab meat and cornflour mixture. Return to a low simmer, stirring constantly until it thickens. Reduce the heat and add the beaten egg in a thin stream, stirring constantly—do not let it come to the boil. Add the soy sauce, lime juice and half the coriander.

Divide the noodles among 4 deep bowls and ladle the soup on top. Garnish with the spring onion (green part) and the remaining coriander leaves.

son-in-law eggs

For those in the know, these are fantastic as a first course. For those unfamiliar with this Thai dish, the idea of deep-fried hard-boiled eggs probably doesn't sound too good. Don't be put off, however; these little eggs are surprisingly tasty, and packed with flavour.

25 g (1 oz) dried tamarind pulp or
  3 tablespoons lemon juice
2 dried long red chillies, about 13 cm
  (5 in) long
vegetable oil for deep-frying
110 g (4 oz) Asian shallots, thinly sliced
6 large hard-boiled eggs, shelled
2 tablespoons fish sauce
5 tablespoons palm or brown sugar

Serves 4

If using dried tamarind pulp, put it into a small bowl with 5 tablespoons of boiling water and let soak for 5 minutes. To help the pulp dissolve, mash it with a spoon or fork. Strain the thick liquid into another bowl and discard the fibres and seeds. (This is not necessary if using lemon juice.)

Cut the chillies into 5 mm ($1/4$ in) pieces with scissors or a knife and discard the seeds. Heat 5 cm (2 in) oil in a wok over medium heat and deep-fry the chillies for a few seconds, taking care not to burn them. Remove with a slotted spoon and drain on paper towels.

In the same oil, deep-fry the shallots for 3–4 minutes over medium heat, until lightly browned. Be careful not to burn them. Remove with a slotted spoon and drain on paper towels.

Use a spoon to slide one egg at a time into the same hot oil. Be careful as the oil may splash. Deep-fry for 10–12 minutes, or until eggs are golden brown all over. Remove with a slotted spoon and drain on paper towels. Keep warm.

Put the tamarind liquid or lemon juice, fish sauce and sugar in a saucepan and simmer over medium heat for 5–7 minutes, stirring until all the sugar has dissolved.

Halve the eggs lengthways and arrange them with the yolk upwards on a serving plate. Drizzle the tamarind sauce over the eggs and sprinkle the crispy chillies and shallots over them. Serve immediately.

honey prawns

2 tablespoons sesame seeds
16 raw large prawns (shrimp)
2 tablespoons cornflour, plus extra
  for dusting
vegetable oil, for deep-frying
3 egg whites
90 g (1/4 cup) honey

Serves 4

Heat a frying pan over low to medium
heat. Add the sesame seeds and dry-fry
for 3–4 minutes, stirring regularly until
golden. Set aside.

Peel and devein the prawns, leaving the
tails intact. Pat them dry with paper towels
and dust with a little cornflour, shaking
off any excess. Fill a large, heavy-based
saucepan or wok one-third full of oil and
heat to 180°C (350°F), or until a cube of
bread dropped in the oil turns brown in
15 seconds.

Beat the egg whites in a clean, dry bowl
until soft peaks form. Add the cornflour
and a pinch of salt and gently whisk until
combined and smooth. Using the tail as a
handle, dip the prawns in the batter, then
slowly lower them into the hot oil. Cook
in batches for 3–4 minutes, or until golden
and the prawns are cooked. Remove with
a slotted spoon, then drain on paper
towels and keep warm.

Put the honey and 2 tablespoons oil in a
saucepan and warm over medium heat for
3 minutes, or until bubbling. Place the
prawns on a large plate and drizzle over
the honey sauce. Sprinkle with the toasted
sesame seeds and serve immediately.

butterfly prawns with ponzu dipping sauce

20 raw large prawns (shrimp), peeled and
  deveined, with tails intact
2 tablespoons cornflour
2 eggs
100 g (11/4 cups) fresh breadcrumbs
vegetable oil, for frying
80 ml (1/3 cup) ponzu sauce or
  60 ml (1/4 cup) light soy sauce combined
  with 1 tablespoon lemon juice

Serves 4–5

Cut down the back of the prawn. Place
each prawn between two layers of plastic
wrap and gently beat to form a cutlet.

Put the cornflour, eggs and breadcrumbs
in separate bowls. Lightly beat the eggs
until frothy. Dip each prawn first into the
cornflour, then into the egg and finally into
the breadcrumbs, fully coating each cutlet.

Pour oil into a shallow saucepan to a depth
of 3 cm (1 in). When hot, fry the cutlets in
batches for 10–15 seconds each side until
golden. Serve with the ponzu sauce.

asparagus with poached quail eggs and lime hollandaise

3 tablespoons virgin olive oil
16 asparagus spears, trimmed
1 teaspoon freshly ground black pepper
6 quail eggs or 2 hen eggs
2 egg yolks
150 g (5 1/2 oz) butter, melted
2 tablespoons lime juice
sprinkle of paprika
good-quality Parmesan cheese shavings

Serves 2 as a starter

Pour half the oil onto a dinner plate and roll the asparagus in it until coated all over. Sprinkle the black pepper over the asparagus—it will stick to the oil.

Put 5 cm (2 in) water in a small, deep frying pan. Bring to the boil, then lower the heat to very low. Crack each quail egg, one at a time, onto a large spoon. Hold the spoon on the surface of the water for 12–15 seconds until the egg white sets, then gently lower the spoon into the water, immersing the egg. Hold for 20–25 seconds until the yolk is firm but still runny. This will take longer if using hen eggs.

Heat the remaining oil in a large frying pan and cook the asparagus over high heat for 2 minutes, or until tender.

To make the hollandaise, whizz the egg yolks in a small food processor and slowly add the melted butter in a thin, steady stream. Mix until fully combined and the sauce is thick and creamy. Add the lime juice and some salt and ground black pepper, if needed.

Divide the asparagus between 2 warmed plates, top with the eggs, drizzle with hollandaise and sprinkle over the paprika. Garnish with the Parmesan cheese shavings and serve immediately.

blini with smoked salmon

200 g (1 1/2 cups) buckwheat flour
125 g (1 cup) plain (all-purpose) flour
2 teaspoons dried yeast
625 ml (2 1/2 cups) warm milk
2 tablespoons melted butter
3 eggs, separated
300 g (10 1/2 oz) smoked salmon, cut into small strips
300 g (10 1/2 oz) sour cream
fresh dill sprigs, to garnish

Makes about 40

Sift the buckwheat and plain flours into a large non-metallic bowl. Add the yeast and 1/2 teaspoon salt and mix well. Make a well in the centre and pour in the warm milk. Mix to a batter and beat for a couple of minutes to get rid of any lumps. Cover the bowl with plastic wrap and leave to rise for 1–2 hours, by which stage it should have formed a bubbly batter.

Using a fork, beat the bubbles out of the batter. Add the melted butter and 3 egg yolks and beat them in. In a separate bowl, whisk the 3 egg whites until stiff peaks form, then gently fold into the batter. Set aside for 10 minutes.

Grease a heavy-based frying pan (or, even better, a blini pan), add spoonfuls of the batter and fry until bubbles rise to the surface and the underside is brown.

Flip the blini over and cook the other side for about 1 minute until brown. Repeat with the rest of the batter. Unless you're planning on an evening feasting solely on blini, you probably won't need the full amount, so freeze any extras; they can be reheated on another occasion.

Keep the blini warm in the oven until you are ready, then serve them with the sour cream, salmon and dill garnish.

deep-fried zucchini flowers

12 zucchini (courgette) flowers, cleaned
50 g (scant 1/2 cup) plain (all-purpose) flour
2 teaspoons olive oil
3 egg whites
vegetable oil, for deep-frying

Serves 4

Trim the zucchini stems to about 2 cm (1 in). To make the batter, sift the flour into a bowl and add a little salt. Add the oil and gently mix with a wooden spoon, then slowly add 75–100 ml (2–3 1/2 fl oz) warm water to make a smooth batter. Whisk the egg whites until stiff peaks form, then fold into the batter.

Fill a deep saucepan one-third full with oil and heat to 180°C (350°F), or until a piece of bread turns brown in 15 seconds.

Holding the stems, gently dip the zucchini flowers into the batter, then carefully add them to the hot oil and fry in batches until golden. Remove with a slotted spoon and drain on paper towels. Serve immediately.

millefeuille of leeks and poached eggs

Millefeuille means 'a thousand leaves' and refers to the many layers of puff pastry. It's a lovely dish but is labour intensive, so best reserve it for a small dinner party.

375 g (13 oz) block puff pastry
1 egg, lightly beaten
6 leeks, white part only
30 g (1 oz) butter
4 very fresh eggs

beurre blanc
50 ml (1¹/2 fl oz) white wine vinegar
125 ml (4 fl oz) white wine
2 shallots, finely chopped
250 g (9 oz) unsalted butter, cubed
salt and white pepper

Serves 4

Preheat the oven to 190°C (375°F/Gas 5). Roll out the pastry on a lightly floured work surface to make a 24 x 12 cm (9¹/2 x 4³/4 in) rectangle. Chill for 10 minutes and then cut into 4 equal triangles. Trim the edges. Transfer to a slightly damp baking tray, lightly brush with the beaten egg and bake for 15 minutes until golden brown. Slice the triangles in half horizontally and use a spoon to remove any uncooked dough. Set aside.

Cut the leeks in half and then into thin julienne strips. Melt the butter in a frying pan, add the leeks and cook, stirring, for 10 minutes until tender. Season with salt.

To poach the eggs, bring 5 cm (2 in) water to the boil. Reduce the heat to very low and, when absolutely still, crack an egg into a bowl or saucer and slide it into the water. Poach for 3 minutes, then remove with a slotted spoon and drain on paper towels. Repeat with the remaining eggs.

To make the beurre blanc, put the white wine vinegar, white wine and shallots into a pan and bring to the boil. Gently simmer to reduce to 3 tablespoons. Strain, then return the mixture to the saucepan. Whisk in the butter, one cube at a time, over low heat, so the butter melts into the sauce and doesn't split. This could take up to 10 minutes. Season the beurre blanc with salt and white pepper.

Arrange the pastry bases on serving plates, top each one with some leek, a poached egg and a little beurre blanc. Cover with the pastry tops and serve with the beurre blanc drizzled around the side.

individual fluffy crab soufflés

Soufflés are considered unpredictable, but they needn't be. The secret lies in beating the egg whites to the right stiffness and serving the soufflé straight from oven to table.

1 1/2 tablespoons butter, melted
4 cloves
1/2 small onion
2 bay leaves
10 black peppercorns
500 ml (2 cups) milk
30 g (1 oz) butter
2 spring onions (scallions), finely chopped
2 tablespoons plain (all-purpose) flour
6 egg yolks and 5 egg whites
250 g (9 oz) cooked crab meat
pinch of cayenne pepper
3 teaspoons lime juice

Serves 6

Preheat the oven to 200°C (400°F/Gas 6). Brush six 125 ml (1/2 cup) ramekins with the melted butter.

Press the cloves into the onion, then put into a small saucepan with the bay leaf, peppercorns and milk. Bring to the boil, then remove from the heat and leave to infuse for 10 minutes. Strain and set aside.

Melt the butter in a heavy-based saucepan, add the spring onions and cook, stirring, for about 3 minutes until softened but not browned. Add the flour and cook, still stirring, for 3 minutes more over low heat.

Remove from the heat and gradually add the milk, stirring after each addition until smooth. Return to the heat and simmer for 3 minutes, stirring constantly. Add the egg yolks, one at a time, beating well with a wooden spoon after each addition. Add the crab meat and stir over medium heat until the mixture is hot and thickens again (do not let it boil). Pour into a large heatproof bowl, then add the cayenne pepper, lime juice, salt and pepper.

Whisk the 5 egg whites in a clean, dry bowl until soft peaks form. Spoon a quarter of the egg white onto the soufflé mixture and quickly but lightly fold it in to loosen the mixture. Incorporate the rest by lifting and folding it in, taking care not to deflate it as you work. Divide the mixture between the ramekins and then run your finger around the inside rim of each ramekin. This helps the soufflés to rise evenly without sticking.

Transfer to a baking tray and bake for 12–15 minutes, or until the soufflés have risen and wobble slightly when tapped. A skewer inserted at the side should come out only slightly moist. Serve immediately.

potato gnocchi with pancetta and basil

1 kg (2 lb 4 oz) floury potatoes, unpeeled
2 egg yolks
2 tablespoons grated Parmesan cheese
125 g (1 cup) plain (all-purpose) flour,
   plus extra, if needed
50 g (1³/4 oz) butter
75 g (2¹/2 oz) pancetta, cut into strips
handful of basil leaves, torn

Serves 4

Preheat the oven to 180°C (350°F/Gas 4).
Prick the potatoes all over, put in a large
roasting tin and bake for 1 hour, or until
tender. Cool for 15 minutes, then peel and
put in a large bowl. Mash by hand.

Add the egg yolks and Parmesan, then
gradually stir in the flour. Work in enough
extra flour to give a very soft, light, pliable
dough. Work with your hands once the
mixture gets too dry to use a spoon. (Do
not overwork the dough, or add too much
extra flour, or the gnocchi will be tough.)
Once a loose dough forms, place on a
lightly floured surface and knead.

Divide the dough into 6 portions. Dust
your hands lightly in flour, then, working
with one portion at a time, roll it out on a
floured work surface to make a rope about
1.5 cm (²/3 in) thick. Cut into 1.5 cm (²/3 in)
lengths. Press your finger into each piece
of dough to form a concave shape, then
use a fork to mark ridges over the outer
surface. Press the edges together. Place
on a floured tray and rest for 10 minutes.

Heat the butter in a frying pan, add the
pancetta and fry until crisp. Set aside.
Bring a large saucepan of salted water to
the boil, then reduce to a simmer. Add the
gnocchi in batches and stir. As the gnocchi
rise to the surface, remove with a slotted
spoon. Divide among bowls. Add the basil
to the pancetta, then spoon over the
gnocchi. Season to taste with pepper.

ziti carbonara

500 g (1 lb 2 oz) ziti or other long
   dried pasta
1 tablespoon olive oil
200 g (7 oz) pancetta, cut into long strips
4 egg yolks
300 ml (10¹/2 fl oz) cream
75 g (³/4 cup) grated Parmesan cheese
2 tablespoons finely chopped flat-leaf
   (Italian) parsley

Serves 4

Cook the pasta in a large saucepan of
rapidly boiling salted water until al dente.
Drain and return to the pan. Meanwhile,
heat the oil in a non-stick frying pan and
cook the pancetta over high heat for
6 minutes, or until crisp and golden.

Put the egg yolks, cream and 50 g (¹/2 cup)
Parmesan in a bowl, mix well, then season.
Pour over the hot pasta in the saucepan
and toss gently. Add the pancetta and
parsley. Cook over very low heat for no
more than 60 seconds, or until the sauce
thickens and coats the pasta. Season with
salt and freshly ground black pepper and
serve at once with the remaining Parmesan.

spaghetti niçoise with fresh seared tuna

This is a fabulous variation on the traditional salad niçoise, and is particularly ideal for casual, vibrant summer dining. Don't skimp on the quality of the ingredients—this is a simple dish and its success lies in the strong flavours of a few key elements.

350 g (12 oz) spaghetti
350 g (12 oz) green beans, trimmed and
   cut into thirds
8 quail eggs, or 4 hen eggs
1 lemon
4 tablespoons olive oil, plus extra
   for brushing
100 g (3 1/2 oz) semi-dried (sun-blushed)
   tomatoes, halved lengthways
50 g (1/3 cup) stoned and halved
   Kalamata olives
3 tablespoons baby capers, drained
3 tablespoons chopped flat-leaf
   (Italian) parsley
350 g (12 oz) fresh tuna steaks

Serves 4

Cook the pasta in a saucepan of boiling water until al dente. Add the beans to the water for the final 4 minutes of cooking. Drain the pasta and beans and set aside.

Meanwhile, put the quail eggs in a clean saucepan of cold water, bring to the boil and cook for 3 minutes (10 minutes for hen eggs). Drain, cool under cold running water, then peel. Cut the quail eggs into halves or the hen eggs into quarters.

Finely grate the zest of the lemon to give 1 teaspoon of grated zest. Squeeze the lemon to give 2 tablespoons juice. Mix the zest and juice with the olive oil and season with salt and freshly ground black pepper. Stir to combine.

Put the tomato pieces, olives, capers and 2 tablespoons of the parsley into a large bowl. Mix together.

To prepare the tuna steaks, lightly brush the tuna with oil, season on both sides and cook on a very hot chargrill or griddle pan, or in a frying pan, until cooked to your liking. (Estimate about 2 minutes per side for medium rare steaks, 4 minutes for well done.) Cut the tuna into 1 cm (1/2 in) thick slices and reserve.

Add the olive and tomato mixture to the pasta and beans. Pour over the lemon juice mixture and toss together. Divide the pasta among serving bowls, arrange the tuna slices on top, garnish with the halved or quartered egg and the remaining chopped parsley, and serve.

egg fried rice with chinese barbecue pork

egg fried rice with chinese barbecue pork

6 spring onions (scallions)
150 g (5^{1}/2 oz) snow peas (mangetout)
200 g (7 oz) Chinese barbecue pork
3 teaspoons sesame oil
2 eggs, lightly beaten
2 garlic cloves, finely chopped
3 cups (about 550 g) cold, cooked white
    long-grain rice (see below)
2 tablespoons soy sauce

Serves 4

Cut the spring onions and snow peas diagonally into very thin shreds. Cut the pork into thin slices.

Heat a wok until hot, add 1 teaspoon of the sesame oil and swirl to coat the base. Add the eggs and swirl over the base until just set. Carefully turn the omelette over and cook for 30 seconds until just lightly browned, then remove from the wok. Allow the egg to cool slightly, then roll up and cut into 1 cm (^{1}/2 in) thick slices.

While the wok is still very hot, add the remaining sesame oil, then the garlic, spring onions and snow peas and stir-fry for 2 minutes, or until slightly soft. Add the pork, rice, soy sauce and strips of omelette and toss until heated through and thoroughly combined—the soy sauce should turn the rice brown. Remove from the heat and serve immediately.

estimating cooked rice
For 3 cups (about 550 g) cooked rice, you need 200 g (1 cup) uncooked long-grain rice. Cook in a large saucepan of boiling water, then drain and spread out on a flat tray to cool. Leave overnight uncovered in the refrigerator.

peppered beef fillet with béarnaise sauce

1 kg (2 lb 4 oz) beef eye fillet, trimmed
1 tablespoon oil
2 garlic cloves, crushed
1 tablespoon cracked black peppercorns
    mixed with 2 teaspoons crushed
    coriander seeds

béarnaise sauce
3 French shallots, finely chopped
125 ml (^{1}/2 cup) dry white wine
2 tablespoons tarragon vinegar
1 tablespoon chopped tarragon
125 g (4^{1}/2 oz) butter
4 egg yolks
1 tablespoon lemon juice

Serves 6

Preheat the oven to 210°C (415°F/Gas 7). Tie the beef fillet at intervals with kitchen string to keep it in shape. Combine the oil and garlic and brush it over the beef, then roll the fillet in the combined peppercorns and coriander seeds.

Sit the meat on a rack in a roasting tin. Bake for 10 minutes, then reduce the heat to 180°C (350°F/Gas 4) and cook for 15–30 minutes more, depending how you like your meat cooked. When ready, cover with foil and rest for 10–15 minutes.

To make the béarnaise sauce, put the shallots, wine, vinegar and chopped tarragon in a saucepan. Boil rapidly until only 2 tablespoons of the liquid remains, then strain it into a bowl. Melt the butter in a small saucepan. Put the wine mixture and egg yolks in a small food processor and blitz for about 30 seconds. With the motor running, add the butter in a thin, steady stream and process until the sauce is thick. Stir in the lemon juice and a pinch of salt and white pepper. Serve the beef with the béarnaise sauce poured over.

steamed salmon parcels with lemon hollandaise sauce

Cooking salmon in its own little parcel ensures the flavour of the fish is retained, blending with (rather than being swamped by) the crisp citrus and salty flavours of the other parcel ingredients. The lemon hollandaise sauce adds an extra tangy note.

3 tablespoons finely chopped flat-leaf
   (Italian) parsley
2 tablespoons small capers
2 teaspoons grated lemon zest
1 tablespoon olive oil
4 skinless salmon fillets, each weighing
   about 175 g (6 oz)
boiled or steamed green beans, to serve

lemon hollandaise
175 g (6 oz) unsalted butter
3 egg yolks
3 tablespoons lemon juice
2 teaspoons white wine vinegar
salt and white pepper

Serves 4

Preheat the oven to 200°C (400°F/Gas 6). Combine the parsley, capers, lemon zest and olive oil in a small bowl and season with salt and freshly ground black pepper. Cut 4 pieces of greaseproof paper, each one large enough to loosely enclose a salmon fillet. Place a fillet in the centre of each piece of paper and season. Spread the parsley mixture over the salmon, then close the parcels and place in a layer on a baking tray. Bake for 15 minutes.

Meanwhile, make the lemon hollandaise. Put the butter into a saucepan and bring to a simmer. Remove from the heat, carefully skim off any scum that rises to the surface, and let cool for 1–2 minutes. Slowly pour the butter into a jug, leaving any whitish sediment behind.

Half-fill a small saucepan with water and bring to a simmer. Put the egg yolks, lemon juice, vinegar and 1 tablespoon water into a medium heatproof bowl and whisk to combine. Place the bowl over the water, making sure that it does not touch the water, and whisk the eggs for 1 minute until thick and foamy.

Gradually add the melted butter, whisking well after each addition. Only add more butter once the mixture has thickened each time. When all the butter has been added, the sauce should leave a trail if the whisk is lifted. Season with salt and white pepper. If the fish isn't ready keep the sauce warm over the pan of water.

Remove the salmon from the parcels, and serve with the hollandaise and beans.

rich snapper pies

3 tablespoons olive oil
2 large red onions, thinly sliced
375 ml (1 1/2 cups) fish stock
600 ml (21 fl oz) cream
1 kg (2 lb 4 oz) skinless snapper fillets,
    cut into 2.5 cm (1 in) pieces
2 hard-boiled eggs, roughly chopped
100 g (3 1/2 oz) peas (defrosted, if frozen)

topping
1.8 kg (4 lb) potatoes, peeled and
    roughly chopped
1 egg, lightly beaten
35 g (1 1/4 oz) grated Parmesan cheese

Serves 6

Heat the oil in a deep frying pan, add the
onions and cook, covered, over low heat
for 20 minutes, stirring occasionally, until
caramelized. Preheat the oven to 200°C
(400°F/Gas 6).

Add the fish stock to the onions, bring to
the boil and cook for about 10 minutes
until the liquid has nearly evaporated. Stir
in the cream and bring to the boil. Reduce
the heat to low and simmer for 20 minutes
until the liquid has reduced by half. Taste,
then season with salt and freshly ground
black pepper if necessary. Set aside.

Meanwhile, put the potatoes in a large
saucepan of boiling salted water and cook
for 15 minutes, or until tender. Drain well.
Return the potatoes to the pan and heat
to evaporate off any liquid. Remove from
the heat and mash coarsely. Add the egg,
half the Parmesan and mash until creamy.

Spoon half the reserved cream sauce into
six 300 ml (10 1/2 fl oz) pie dishes (or one
1.8 litre/7 cup pie dish). Divide the fish,
egg and peas between the dishes, then
spoon over the remaining sauce, leaving a
small gap at the top. Top with the mashed
potato. Sprinkle over the cheese and bake
for 30–40 minutes, or until golden.

lamb and egg koftas in spicy sauce

Snacks of spicy minced lamb, hand-shaped around hard-boiled eggs, are found in many cultures. This Indian version is known as *nargisi kofta*, a reference to the similarity of the cooked and halved kofta with the almond-shaped narcissus flower. Well, you can but try.

10 small hen eggs, or quail eggs
1 onion, finely chopped
4 garlic cloves, crushed
1 teaspoon salt
1/2 teaspoon ground turmeric
1 teaspoon garam masala
1 teaspoon chilli powder
550 g (1 lb 4 oz) minced (ground) lamb
3 tablespoons rice flour, for dusting
vegetable oil, for deep-frying

spicy tomato sauce
2 large ripe tomatoes
1 tablespoon oil
1 onion, thinly sliced
2 garlic cloves, chopped
2.5 cm (1 in) piece of fresh ginger, grated
1 teaspoon ground turmeric
1 teaspoon salt
1 teaspoon garam masala
1/2 teaspoon sugar
1/2 teaspoon chilli powder (optional)
125 ml (1/2 cup) thick natural yoghurt

Serves 4

To make the koftas, cook 8 of the eggs in boiling water for 10 minutes until hard-boiled, then cool them immediately under cold running water to prevent grey rings around the yolks. When cold, peel.

Mix the onion, garlic, salt, turmeric, garam masala and chilli powder in a large bowl. Add the lamb and knead together with your hands. Beat 1 of the remaining eggs in a bowl and knead it into the mince.

Divide into 8 portions and shape each one into a ball. Flatten a ball into a pancake on the palm of your hand and place a hard-boiled egg in the centre. Wrap the mixture around the egg, smoothly and evenly. Make the rest, then dust with rice flour.

Fill a deep heavy-based saucepan one-third full with oil and heat to 180°C/350°F, or until a cube of bread browns in about 15 seconds. Beat the remaining egg with a little water. One by one, dip each kofta into the egg, shake off any excess, then deep-fry until golden. Drain on paper towels.

To make the sauce, score a cross in the top of each tomato, put into boiling water for 20 seconds, then plunge into cold water. Drain, peel the skin away from the cross, then chop the flesh, discarding the cores and seeds and reserving the juices.

Heat the oil in a saucepan and fry the onion, garlic and ginger for 5 minutes. Stir in the turmeric, salt, garam masala, sugar and chilli powder, if using, and the tomato. Simmer for a few minutes, then stir in the yoghurt and 125 ml (1/2 cup) hot water. Simmer for 5 minutes, then season. Slice the koftas in half, add the sauce and serve.

roast vegetable melt with poached egg

4 tablespoons olive oil
6 baby onions or French shallots, peeled
1 bundle of asparagus, cut into 5 cm (2 in) pieces
2 zucchini (courgettes), thickly sliced
1 eggplant (aubergine), cubed
4 garlic cloves, peeled
1 tablespoon lemon juice
2 eggs
125 g (4^{1}/$_{2}$ oz) Camembert cheese, roughly cubed

Serves 2

Preheat the oven to 200°C (400°F/Gas 6). Put the oil in a large roasting tin and add the onions, asparagus, zucchini, eggplant and garlic. Season with salt and freshly ground black pepper and toss together. Roast the vegetables for 20 minutes, sprinkle over the lemon juice, and roast for a further 10 minutes.

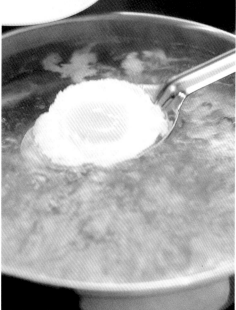

Put 5 cm (2 in) water in a large saucepan and bring to the boil. When the water is bubbling, turn the heat down as low as possible. Crack an egg into a small bowl or saucer and very gently slip the egg into the water—the white should start to turn opaque almost as soon as it hits the water. Repeat with the other egg, keeping them separate. Don't worry if the egg whites spread out in the water. Leave the eggs undisturbed for 3 minutes, then remove with a slotted spoon.

Divide the vegetables between 2 small ovenproof dishes. Scatter the Camembert cheese over the vegetables, dividing it evenly. Return the dishes to the oven for 1–2 minutes, to melt the cheese a little. Remove, top each dish with a poached egg and some freshly ground black pepper, and serve.

the sweet egg

If there is a realm where eggs *really* excel, it has to be desserts. They seem to go well with everything, be it fruit and nuts or chocolate, coffee and alcohol. Nor does the season phase them: mini meringues topped with mango and passionfruit are perfect in summer, but chocolate and Frangelico mousse is ideal for cold, wintery nights.

praline semifreddo

200 g (7 oz) blanched almonds
200 g (scant 1 cup) caster
   (superfine) sugar
600 ml (21 fl oz) thick
   (double/heavy) cream
2 eggs, separated
100 g (generous 3/4 cup) icing
   (confectioners') sugar, sifted
2 tablespoons Mandorla (almond-
   flavoured Marsala) or brandy

Serves 6

To make the praline, put the blanched
almonds in a hot frying pan and dry-fry
until brown all over, then set aside. Melt
the sugar in a saucepan over medium
heat until golden, tipping the saucepan
from side to side so that the sugar melts
evenly. Remove the pan from the heat and
add the almonds. Toss to mix. Pour on to
a greased baking tray and smooth out
with the back of a spoon. Leave to cool.

Meanwhile, pour the cream into a large
bowl and whisk until soft peaks form. When
the praline has cooled, finely crush it in a
food processor or use a rolling pin or
pestle and mortar.

Beat the egg yolks with a quarter of the
icing sugar until pale. In a clean, dry glass
bowl, whisk the egg whites until stiff peaks
form, then gradually add the rest of the
icing sugar and whisk until glossy, stiff
peaks form. Gently fold the egg yolks into
the cream, then fold in the egg whites.
Fold in the praline and Mandorla.

Spoon the mixture into six 250 ml (1 cup)
metal dariole moulds. Level the surface
and tap each mould on the bench a few
times. Cover the surface with foil and
freeze for at least 24 hours. To unmould,
leave the moulds at room temperature for
5 minutes. Dip the bases briefly into hot
water, then run a knife around the edge.
Invert onto serving plates.

coffee gelato

5 egg yolks
115 g (1/2 cup) sugar
500 ml (2 cups) milk
125 ml (1/2 cup) freshly made espresso
1 tablespoon Tia Maria or coffee liqueur

Serves 6

Whisk the egg yolks and half the sugar in
a bowl until you have a pale and creamy
mixture. Pour the milk and coffee into a
saucepan, add the remaining sugar and
bring to the boil. Add to the egg mixture
and whisk together. Pour back into the
saucepan and cook over low heat, taking
care that the custard doesn't boil. Stir
constantly until the mixture is thick enough
to coat the back of a wooden spoon.
Strain the custard into a bowl and cool
over ice before adding the Tia Maria.

To make the gelato by hand, pour the
mixture into a freezerproof container, cover
and freeze. Every 30 minutes break up the
ice crystals with a fork to ensure a smooth
texture. Repeat until it is ready—this may
take 4 hours. If using an ice cream machine,
follow the manufacturer's instructions.

frozen zabaglione with marsala sauce

There's no getting away from the fact that this sumptuous Italian dessert and sauce is very rich and probably not good for you. But, that's exactly what you want when entertaining, and this frozen version means that much can be done in advance.

170 ml (2/3 cup) thick
  (double/heavy) cream
4 egg yolks
1 teaspoon pure vanilla extract
170 ml (2/3 cup) sweet Marsala
4 tablespoons caster (superfine) sugar

Serves 4

Whisk the cream until firm peaks form, then cover and refrigerate.

Put the egg yolks, vanilla, half the Marsala and half the sugar in a large non-metallic bowl and whisk together.

Sit the bowl on top of a saucepan one-third full of simmering water, ensuring that the base of the bowl does not touch the water. Using an electric whisk, whisk constantly for 5 minutes, or until foamy and thick enough that it holds its form when drizzled from the whisk (if using a hand whisk, this will take longer).

Remove the bowl from the heat and sit in another bowl of ice. Whisk the mixture until cool, then remove from the ice and gently fold in the whipped cream. Pour the mixture into four 125 ml (1/2 cup) dariole moulds or ramekins, cover with plastic wrap and freeze until firm. This may take up to 6 hours.

Put the remaining Marsala and sugar in a small saucepan and stir over low heat until the sugar dissolves. Bring to the boil, then reduce the heat and simmer for 5 minutes, or until just syrupy. Remove from the heat and cool.

Briefly dip the moulds into warm water, then loosen with a knife. Carefully invert the zabaglione onto plates and drizzle over the syrup. Serve at once.

baked alaska

baked alaska

2 litres (8 cups) good-quality vanilla
  ice cream
250 g (9 oz) mixed glacé fruit, finely
  chopped
125 ml (^{1}/2 cup) Grand Marnier
  or Cointreau
2 teaspoons grated orange zest
60 g (2^1/4 oz) toasted almonds,
  finely chopped
60 g (2^1/4 oz) good-quality dark
  chocolate, finely chopped
1 sponge or butter cake, about 350 g
  (12 oz), cut into 3 cm (1^1/4 in) slices
3 egg whites
185 g (generous ^{3}/4 cup) caster
  (superfine) sugar

Serves 6–8

Line a 2 litre (8 cup) pudding basin with
damp muslin. Allow half of the ice cream
to soften just enough that you can fold in
the glacé fruit along with 2 tablespoons of
the liqueur and 1 teaspoon of the orange
zest. Spoon the ice cream over the base
and up the sides of the basin, then freeze
until hard.

Soften the remaining ice cream and fold in
the almonds, dark chocolate, remaining
liqueur and orange zest. Add to the frozen
shell, filling it and smoothing the surface.
Working quickly, evenly cover the ice
cream with a layer of cake. Cover with foil
and freeze for 2 hours.

Preheat the oven to 220°C (425°F/Gas 7).
Beat the egg whites until soft peaks form.
Gradually add the sugar, beating well after
each addition. Beat for 4–5 minutes, until
thick and glossy.

Carefully unmould the ice cream onto a
flat ovenproof dish and gently remove the
muslin. Quickly spread the meringue over
the top, completely covering the ice
cream. Bake for 5–8 minutes until lightly
browned. Serve immediately.

blackberry bavarois

225 g (8 oz) blackberries
50 ml (scant ^{1}/4 cup) blackberry syrup
1 tablespoon lemon juice
150 g (^{2}/3 cup) caster (superfine) sugar
450 ml (16 fl oz) milk
^{1}/2 teaspoon pure vanilla extract
5 egg yolks
6 sheets leaf gelatine or 3 teaspoons
  powdered gelatine
200 ml (7 fl oz) pouring cream
extra blackberries, to garnish

Serves 6

Purée the blackberries, syrup, lemon juice
and 25 g (1 oz) sugar until smooth, then
pass through a fine strainer and chill.

Put the milk and vanilla extract in a large
saucepan and heat until just below boiling
point. Beat the egg yolks and remaining
sugar until thick and pale. Gradually whisk
in the hot milk. Pour into a clean pan and
stir constantly over low heat until the
custard thickens and a line drawn across
the back of a wooden spoon holds its
shape. Remove the custard from the heat.

Soak the gelatine sheets in a bowl of cold
water until soft, then remove and squeeze
out any excess water with your hands.
Whisk the gelatine into the hot custard
mixture until dissolved. (If using powdered
gelatine, place in a bowl and add 60 ml
(^{1}/4 cup) water. Stir quickly to dissolve,
then add to the custard and mix well.)
Strain though a sieve, then cool to room
temperature by placing over a bowl of
iced water. Add the blackberry purée and
stir through.

Whip the cream until soft peaks form, then
fold through the blackberry mixture until
combined. Pour into six 185 ml (^{3}/4 cup)
ramekins and chill for 4 hours, or until set.
Unmould by running a knife around the
edge, then turn out and garnish with the
extra blackberries.

chocolate and frangelico mousse

90 g (3¼ oz) dark chocolate, chopped
1 tablespoon unsalted butter
2 tablespoons Frangelico
2 eggs, separated
250 ml (1 cup) cream, whipped
70 g (2½ oz) white chocolate

Serves 6

Put the dark chocolate, butter and
Frangelico in a heatproof bowl set over a
small saucepan of simmering water, making
sure the bowl does not touch the water.
Gently stir the chocolate occasionally until
melted, then remove from the heat and let
cool slightly. Lightly beat the egg yolks,
then stir them into the melted chocolate.
Gently fold in the cream until velvety.

Beat the egg whites until soft peaks form.
Using a metal spoon, fold one spoonful
into the mousse, then gently fold in the
remainder. Use a light, quick touch. Spoon
the mousse into six small 175 ml (⅔ cup)
cappuccino cups, glasses or ramekins.
Cover with plastic wrap and refrigerate for
at least 4 hours, though ideally overnight,
until set.

Just before serving, make the white
chocolate curls. Grate the chocolate into
long thin curls, then sprinkle them on top
of the mousses and serve.

entertaining ideas
If you prefer, serve the mousse in brandy-
snap baskets, available from supermarkets
and delicatessens.

pears poached in wine with sabayon

Sabayon is the French word for zabaglione, the famous frothy creation based on sugar, egg yolks and wine. It is normally a dessert but can be a sauce, as it is here. In this version, the light, sweet flavour of the sabayon enhances the delicate flavour of the pear.

500 ml (2 cups) dry white wine
60 g (1/4 cup) caster (superfine) sugar
1 vanilla pod, split
2 tablespoons orange juice
4 firm, ripe pears
2 egg yolks
60 ml (1/4 cup) double cream, lightly
  whipped and chilled

Serves 4

Put the wine, sugar, vanilla pod and orange juice in a large saucepan or frying pan and bring gently to the boil, stirring occasionally to dissolve the sugar. Boil for 2 minutes, then set aside.

Peel and halve the pears, then remove the cores. Put the pears in a single layer in the pan, then cover and gently simmer for 5 minutes. Turn the pears over and cook for 5 minutes more, or until tender when pierced with the tip of a knife. Remove from the heat and leave to cool.

Remove the pears from the liquid and set aside. Strain the poaching liquid into a jug and pour 300 ml (10 1/2 fl oz) of the liquid into a saucepan (if you have less than that, use whatever is left). Bring gently to the boil, lower the heat and simmer for about 20 minutes until the liquid is reduced by two-thirds.

Put the egg yolks in a bowl and briefly beat with electric beaters. Still beating, add the reduced liquid, pouring it slowly down one side of the bowl. Whisk for 5 minutes, or until cold. Fold in the chilled cream and chill for up to 2 hours, then serve it spooned over the pears.

crème caramel

230 g (1 cup) caster (superfine) sugar
650 ml (22 fl oz) milk
3 eggs, plus 3 yolks
1 teaspoon pure vanilla extract

Makes 6

Preheat the oven to 150°C (300°F/Gas 2). To make the caramel, dissolve half the sugar in 60 ml (1/4 cup) water in a heavy-based saucepan over medium heat. Boil the syrup steadily, tipping (not stirring) the saucepan from side to side occasionally to ensure a deep golden colour. Remove the pan from the heat. One at a time, carefully pour the caramel into six 175 ml (2/3 cup) ramekins, turning each ramekin to coat the sides. Do this quickly before the caramel sets. Put the ramekins in a deep baking tray and set aside.

Put the milk in a small pan and bring to just below boiling point. Put the whole eggs, yolks, remaining sugar and vanilla extract in a bowl and whisk until just combined. Slowly strain the milk over the eggs, stirring constantly with a wooden spoon. Use a gentle action to minimize disturbance. Strain the mixture into a jug and allow to settle for 3–4 minutes. Carefully skim off any air bubbles that have risen to the surface. (This will help ensure the custards have a smooth, velvety finish.)

Very carefully ladle the mixture into the ramekins, working quickly to avoid creating any more air bubbles. Pour enough hot water into the tray to come halfway up the outside of the ramekins. Bake for 1 hour, or until just firm to the touch. Carefully transfer the custards to a wire rack and refrigerate overnight.

To serve, dip the ramekins in a small bowl of boiling water, then run a knife around the edges to loosen the custard. Invert the custards onto serving dishes and pour over any leftover caramel.

crème brûlée

In English, this dish translates as 'burnt cream', an apt enough description, but not really evoking the glory that is a good crème brûlée. It has the same smooth, custardy flavour of a crème caramel, but with the added sweetness of the caramelized topping.

600 ml (20½ fl oz) cream
5 cm (2 in) piece of lemon zest, white pith removed
80 g (⅓ cup) caster (superfine) sugar, plus extra to glaze
1 vanilla bean, split
5 egg yolks

Serves 6

Preheat the oven to 140°C (275°F/Gas 1). Put the cream, lemon and half the sugar in a saucepan. Scrape the vanilla seeds out of the pod and add to the pan, along with the pod. Bring to just below boiling point over medium heat, stirring constantly to dissolve the sugar. Remove the pan from the heat and allow to infuse for 10 minutes.

Whisk the egg yolks and remaining sugar in a bowl. Very slowly pour the cream over the egg mixture, stirring constantly but gently to minimize disturbance. Strain the mixture into a jug and carefully skim the surface of any air bubbles.

Pour the custard into six 125 ml (½ cup) ramekins and carefully transfer to a deep baking tray. Add enough hot water to the tray to reach halfway up the outside of the ramekins, then cook for 1 hour, or until the custard has set and is slightly wobbly.

Remove from the oven and transfer the ramekins to a wire rack. When completely cool, refrigerate for at least 4 hours.

Preheat the grill (broiler) to very hot. Sprinkle 1–2 teaspoons of the extra caster sugar over the top of each brûlée, brushing any sugar off the rim as it will burn under the grill.

Place the ramekins in a roasting tin full of ice, then place the tin under the grill for 4 minutes, or until the tops of the brûlées have caramelized. Refrigerate for up to 30 minutes, then serve.

berry soufflé with warm berry sauce

What this dish might cost you in nervous energy, it will repay in full when you carry it triumphantly to the table. Make the sauce in advance and reheat it while the soufflés cook.

55 g (2 oz) butter
3 tablespoons plain (all-purpose) flour
250 ml (1 cup) milk
115 g (1/2 cup) caster (superfine) sugar,
  plus extra for sprinkling
1/2 teaspoon salt
250 g (9 oz) berries, such as blackberries,
  raspberries or blueberries, or a mixture
1 tablespoon berry-flavoured liqueur
  or brandy such as framboise eau de
  vie (optional)
4 egg yolks
6 egg whites
icing (confectioners') sugar, for dusting

warm berry sauce
100 g (generous 1/3 cup) caster
  (superfine) sugar
300 g (10 1/2 oz) frozen mixed berries,
  such as blackberries, raspberries or
  blueberries (defrosted, juice retained)
1 tablespoon berry-flavoured liqueur
  or brandy such as framboise eau de vie

Serves 6

Preheat the oven to 190°C (375°F/Gas 5). Melt the butter in a saucepan over low heat. Use a little of it to brush the insides of six 250 ml (1 cup) soufflé dishes, then sprinkle them with a little caster sugar. Shake the dishes to coat them evenly in the sugar. Tip out any excess.

Return the remaining butter to the heat. Add the flour to the pan and cook for 1 minute, stirring until it begins to change colour and thickens a little. Remove from the heat and gradually add the milk, stirring constantly. Stir in the sugar and salt. Return to low heat and whisk until it is smooth and has come to the boil.

Remove from the heat and allow to cool for 5 minutes. Meanwhile, purée the mixed berries until smooth, then sieve to remove any seeds. Add to the milk mixture, along with the liqueur, if using. Mix well.

Lightly beat the egg yolks, then beat into the berry mixture until smooth. Whisk the egg whites in a clean, dry bowl until stiff peaks form. With a metal spoon, fold one-quarter of the whites through the base mixture to loosen it slightly. Gently fold in the remaining egg whites. Spoon the soufflé mixture into the prepared dishes. Smooth the top and run a finger around the edge of each dish to help the soufflés rise evenly. Bake for 13–15 minutes, or until well risen and firm to touch.

Meanwhile, make the berry sauce. Put the sugar and 100 ml (3 1/2 fl oz) water in a pan and bring to the boil to dissolve the sugar. Boil for 2 minutes. Add the berries and liqueur or brandy. Reduce the heat and simmer for 10 minutes. Cool slightly. Serve the berry soufflés immediately, dusted with icing sugar and the sauce poured over.

lemon pudding with citrus cream

60 g (2 oz) butter, softened
185 g (generous 3/4 cup) sugar
2 teaspoons grated lemon zest
3 eggs, separated
30 g (1/4 cup) self-raising flour
185 ml (3/4 cup) milk
80 ml (1/3 cup) lemon juice

citrus cream
300 ml (10 1/2 fl oz) thick
   (double/heavy) cream
2 tablespoons icing (confectioners') sugar
grated zest of 1 orange
grated zest of 1/2 lime

Serves 4–6

Preheat the oven to 180°C (350°F/Gas 4).
Lightly grease a 1 litre (4 cup) ovenproof
or soufflé dish. Put the butter, sugar and
lemon zest in a bowl and beat until light
and well combined.

Add the egg yolks gradually, beating well
after each addition. Add the flour and
milk alternately to make a smooth but not
runny batter. Stir in the lemon juice. The
batter may look to have separated at this
stage, but this is fine.

In a separate bowl, whisk the egg whites
until firm but not dry peaks form, then use
a metal spoon to gently fold the whites
into the batter. Pour the batter into the
ovenproof dish and place in a roasting tin.
Fill the tin with enough boiling water to
come one-third of the way up the outside
of the dish. Cook for 40–45 minutes, or
until risen and firm to the touch. Allow to
stand for 10 minutes before serving.

Meanwhile, make the citrus cream. Whip
the cream with the sugar until soft peaks
form. Fold in the grated orange and lime
zest. Dust the pudding with icing sugar, if
you like, and serve with the citrus cream.

fig and raspberry cake

185 g (6 1/4 oz) unsalted butter
185 g (generous 3/4 cup) caster (superfine)
   sugar, plus extra for sprinkling
1 egg, plus 1 egg yolk
335 g (2 2/3 cups) plain (all-purpose) flour
1 teaspoon baking powder
4 figs, quartered
grated zest of 1 orange
200 g (7 oz) raspberries

Serves 6

Preheat the oven to 180°C (350°F/Gas 4).
Lightly grease a 23 cm (9 in) springform tin.
Cream the butter and sugar until light. Add
the egg and yolk and beat again. Sift in the
flour, baking powder and pinch of salt, and
combine to form a dough. Chill until firm.

Divide the dough in two and roll out one
piece large enough to cover the base of
the tin. Place in the prepared tin, gently
pressing the dough up the sides a little.
Cover with the figs, orange zest and
raspberries. Roll out the remaining dough
and place it over the filling. Brush with
water and sprinkle with a little sugar. Bake
for 30 minutes and serve warm.

chocolate croissant pudding

chocolate croissant pudding

4 croissants, torn into pieces
125 g (4 1/2 oz) good-quality dark
   chocolate, chopped into pieces
4 eggs
100 g (scant 1/2 cup) caster
   (superfine) sugar
250 ml (1 cup) milk
250 ml (1 cup) cream
3 teaspoons orange liqueur
1 teaspoon grated orange zest
4 tablespoons orange juice
2 tablespoons roughly chopped hazelnuts
cream, for serving

Serves 6–8

Preheat the oven to 180°C (350°F/Gas 4).
Grease the base and side of a 20 cm (8 in)
deep-sided cake tin and line the bottom
of the tin with baking paper. Put the
croissant pieces into the tin, then scatter
over 100 g (3 1/2 oz) chocolate pieces.

Beat the eggs and sugar together until
pale and creamy. Heat the milk, cream,
liqueur and remaining chocolate pieces
in a saucepan until almost boiling. Stir to
melt the chocolate, then remove the pan
from the heat. Gradually add to the egg
mixture, stirring constantly. Next, stir in
the orange zest and juice. Slowly pour the
mixture over the croissants, allowing time
for the liquid to be fully absorbed before
adding more.

Sprinkle the hazelnuts over the top and
bake for 50 minutes, or until a skewer
comes out clean when inserted into the
centre. Cool for 10 minutes. Turn the
pudding out and invert onto a serving
plate. Slice and serve warm with a dollop
of cream.

individual sticky date cakes

270 g (1 1/2 cups) pitted dates, chopped
1 teaspoon bicarbonate of soda
150 g (5 1/2 oz) unsalted butter, chopped
185 g (1 1/2 cups) self-raising flour
265 g (generous 1 cup) firmly packed soft
   brown sugar
2 eggs, lightly beaten
2 tablespoons golden syrup (dark
   corn syrup)
185 ml (3/4 cup) pouring cream

Makes 6

Preheat the oven to 180°C (350°F/Gas 4).
Grease six 250 ml (1 cup) muffin tin holes.
Put the dates and 250 ml (1 cup) water in
a saucepan, bring to the boil, then remove
from the heat and stir in the bicarbonate
of soda. Add 60 g (1/4 cup) of the butter
and stir until melted.

Sift the flour into a large bowl, then stir in
125 g (generous 1/2 cup) of the sugar.
Make a well in the centre, add the date
mixture and eggs and stir until combined.
Evenly divide the mixture among the
muffin holes and bake for 20 minutes, or
until a skewer comes out clean when
inserted into the centre.

To make the sauce, put the golden syrup,
cream, the remaining butter and sugar in
a small saucepan and stir over low heat for
about 4 minutes, or until the sugar has
dissolved. Bring to the boil, then reduce
the heat and simmer, stirring occasionally,
for 2 minutes.

To serve, put the warm cakes onto serving
plates, pierce a few times with a skewer
and drizzle over the sauce. Serve with ice
cream, if desired.

mini fruit flans

185 g (1¹/2 cups) plain (all-purpose) flour
2 tablespoons caster (superfine) sugar
125 g (4¹/2 oz) unsalted butter, diced
2–3 tablespoons iced water

fruit filling
3 egg yolks
3 tablespoons caster (superfine) sugar
2 tablespoons plain (all-purpose) flour
250 ml (1 cup) milk
1 teaspoon pure vanilla extract
1 punnet small strawberries, halved
2 ripe nectarines, thinly sliced
80 g (¹/4 cup) apricot jam, to glaze

Makes 6

Put the flour, sugar and butter in a food processor and, using the pulse button in short bursts, mix until it resembles fine breadcrumbs. Add the water and process until the dough just comes together.

Turn out and press into a ball, then roll out to fit six 10 cm (4 in) mini fluted cake tins, 2 cm (1 in) deep. Line the tins, trim off excess pastry and chill for 30 minutes. Preheat the oven to 190°C (375°F/Gas 5).

Prick the bottoms of the pastry shells with a fork, then line them with baking paper and fill with baking beads or uncooked rice. Bake for 10 minutes, then remove the paper and beads or rice and bake for a further 20 minutes until cooked. Cool.

To make the filling, whisk the yolks and sugar until light and creamy, then whisk in the flour. Bring the milk to the boil, then slowly add to the egg mixture, whisking constantly. Pour into a clean pan, return to the boil over medium heat, and whisk until thick. Transfer to a bowl, add the vanilla, and cool to room temperature, stirring often. Cover with plastic wrap and chill. Spoon the custard into the pastry shells, then top with the fruit. Heat the jam, strain and brush over for a shiny glaze.

tarte au citron

If you have never made your own pastry before, this classic tart is a good place to start. The techniques themselves are so satisfying—working in the flour, kneading and rolling out the dough—that the smell of pastry baking and the lemony filling are added extras.

350 g (generous 2¹/3 cups) plain
   (all-purpose) flour
150 g (5¹/2 oz) unsalted butter, cubed
100 g (generous ³/4 cup) icing
   (confectioners') sugar
2 eggs, beaten

lemon filling
4 eggs
2 egg yolks
275 g (scant 1¹/4 cups) caster
   (superfine) sugar
190 ml (6¹/2 fl oz) thick
   (double/heavy) cream
275 ml (9¹/2 fl oz) lemon juice
finely grated zest of 3 lemons

Serves 8

To make the pastry, sift the flour and a pinch of salt into a bowl. Add the butter and work in, using your fingertips and thumb, until it is very soft. Add the sugar and mix in with a wooden spoon. Add the eggs and mix together, initially with the spoon, then, once the dough starts to come together, with your hands.

Transfer to a clean work surface and knead a few times to make a smooth dough. Roll into a ball, wrap in plastic wrap and chill for at least 1 hour.

Preheat the oven to 190°C (375°F/Gas 5). Roll out the pastry to line a 28 cm (11 in) round, loose-based fluted tart tin. Trim the edge and pinch up the pastry edge to make an even border. Chill for 20 minutes. To make the filling, whisk together the eggs, yolks and sugar. Add the cream, still whisking, then the lemon juice and zest.

Line the pastry shell with a piece of baking paper and baking beads or uncooked rice. Blind bake the pastry for 10 minutes, remove the paper and beads or rice and bake for 3–5 minutes more. Remove from the oven and reduce the temperature to 150°C (300°F/Gas 2).

Put the tin on a baking tray and carefully pour the filling into the pastry case, letting it settle evenly. Return to the oven for 35–40 minutes, or until the filling has set. Leave to cool completely before serving.

new york cheesecake

The cheesecake goes back a long way. The ancient Romans baked cheese into tiny cakes, and written recipes for it date back to the Middle Ages. Fast forward to the present and we have what many consider to be the final word on the matter: the New York cheesecake.

60 g (1/2 cup) self-raising flour
125 g (1 cup) plain (all-purpose) flour
3 tablespoons caster (superfine) sugar
1 teaspoon grated lemon zest
80 g (2 3/4 oz) unsalted butter, diced
1 egg
icing (confectioners') sugar and whipped
   cream (optional), to serve

the filling

750 g (1 lb 10 oz) cream cheese, softened
230 g (1 cup) caster (superfine) sugar
3 tablespoons plain (all-purpose) flour
2 teaspoons grated orange zest
2 teaspoons grated lemon zest
4 eggs
170 ml (2/3 cup) cream, whipped

Serves 10–12

Briefly process the flours, sugar, zest and butter in a food processor until crumbly. Add the egg and process until the mixture just comes together. Turn out onto a lightly floured work surface and gather together into a ball. Wrap in plastic wrap and chill for about 20 minutes, or until the dough is firm.

Preheat the oven to 210°C (415°F/Gas 7). Lightly grease a 23 cm (9 in) springform tin. Roll out the dough between 2 sheets of baking paper until large enough to fit the base and side of the tin. Ease into the tin and trim the edges. Line the pastry with baking paper and add baking beads or uncooked rice. Bake for 10 minutes, then remove the baking paper and beads or rice. Flatten the pastry lightly with the back of a spoon and bake for a further 5 minutes. Set aside to cool.

To make the filling, reduce the oven to 150°C (300°F/Gas 2). Beat the cream cheese, sugar, flour and citrus zest until smooth. Beat in the eggs, one at a time, then the cream. Pour into the pastry base and bake for 1 3/4 hours until almost set. Turn off the oven and leave to cool with the door ajar. When cool, remove the cheesecake and chill completely in the refrigerator. Dust with icing sugar and serve with whipped cream, if wished.

chocolate and almond torte

Any dessert that features chocolate, mascarpone cheese and a dash of brandy is pretty much destined for success. What will ensure return visits is the quality of the ingredients. In particular, buy good-quality chocolate—it will make a difference.

150 g (5^1/2 oz) flaked or whole almonds
1 slice pandoro sweet cake or 1 small
   brioche (about 40 g/1^1/2 oz)
300 g (10^1/2 oz) good-quality
   dark chocolate
2 tablespoons brandy
150 g (5^1/2 oz) unsalted butter, softened
150 g (^{2}/3 cup) caster (superfine) sugar
4 eggs
200 g (7 oz) mascarpone cheese
1 teaspoon pure vanilla extract (optional)
cocoa powder, to dust
crème fraîche or sour cream, to serve

Serves 8

Preheat the oven to 170°C (325°F/Gas 4). Toast the almonds in the oven for about 8 minutes until golden brown, watching to ensure they do not burn.

Put the almonds and pandoro or brioche in a food processor and process until the mixture resembles coarse breadcrumbs. Alternatively, finely chop the nuts and pandoro and mix them together. Lightly grease a 23 cm (9 in) springform tin. Tip some of the mixture into the tin and shake it around so that it forms a coating on the bottom and side of the tin. Set aside the remaining nut mixture.

Gently melt the chocolate and brandy in a heatproof bowl set over a saucepan of simmering water, taking care that the bowl does not touch the water and that no water gets into the bowl. Stir occasionally until the chocolate has completely melted. Allow to cool slightly.

Cream the butter and sugar in the food processor (or in a bowl with a wooden spoon) for a few minutes until light and pale. Add the melted chocolate, eggs, mascarpone, vanilla and the remaining nut mixture. Mix well, then tip into the tin.

Bake for 50–60 minutes, or until just set. Leave the torte to rest in the tin for about 15 minutes before removing. Dust with a little cocoa when cool and serve with crème fraîche.

almond friands

150 g (5¹/2 oz) unsalted butter
90 g (1 cup) flaked almonds
4 tablespoons plain (all-purpose) flour
165 g (1¹/3 cups) icing (confectioners')
  sugar, plus extra, to dust
5 egg whites

Makes 10

Preheat the oven to 210°C (415°F/Gas 7).
Lightly grease ten 125 ml (¹/2 cup) friand
tins. Melt the butter in a small saucepan
over medium heat, then cook until the
butter turns a deep golden colour—this
should take only a couple of minutes.
Remove the pan from the heat and strain
to remove any residue (the colour will
deepen on standing). Set aside to cool.

Blitz the almonds in a food processor until
finely ground. Put into a bowl and sift the
flour and icing sugar into the same bowl.

Put the egg whites in a separate bowl and
whisk with a fork until just combined and
bubbles form. Add to the flour mixture,
along with the butter. Mix together with
a metal spoon until well combined.

Sit the friand tins on a baking tray then
pour the batter into each tin until it is
three-quarters full. Bake in the centre of
the oven for 10 minutes, then reduce the
heat to 180°C (350°F/Gas 4) and bake for
a further 5 minutes. To test for doneness,
insert a skewer into the centre of a friand.
If it comes out clean, they are ready. (They
should also split across the top slightly.)

Remove from the oven and leave to cool
in the tins for 5 minutes before turning out
onto a wire rack and cooling completely.
Dust with icing sugar, then serve.

double chocolate brownies

4 tablespoons butter
40 g (¹/₃ cup) cocoa powder
145 g (²/₃ cup) caster (superfine) sugar
2 eggs
60 g (¹/₂ cup) plain (all-purpose) flour
¹/₂ teaspoon baking powder
100 g (¹/₂ cup) chocolate chips

Makes 12

Preheat the oven to 180°C (350°F/Gas 4). Grease a 16 cm (6 in) square tin and line with baking paper.

Over a low heat, melt the butter in a saucepan. When ready, remove from the heat and stir in the cocoa and sugar, then add the eggs.

Place a sieve over the saucepan and tip in the flour and baking powder, along with a pinch of salt. Sift into the saucepan, then mix it in thoroughly. Add the chocolate chips and stir them in.

Pour the mixture into the tin and bake for 30 minutes, or until a skewer inserted into the centre comes out clean. Leave the cake to cool in the tin, then tip out and cut it into brownie pieces.

italian orange biscuits

175 g (generous 1¹/₃ cups) plain (all-purpose) flour
200 g (1¹/₃ cups) semolina or fine polenta
100 g (generous ¹/₃ cup) caster (superfine) sugar
100 g (3¹/₂ oz) unsalted butter, softened
2¹/₂ teaspoons grated orange zest
2 eggs

Makes 20

Put the flour, semolina, sugar, butter, zest, eggs and a pinch of salt in a food processor and mix until smooth. Chill for 15 minutes.

Preheat the oven to 180°C (350°F/Gas 4). Grease a baking tray and roll tablespoons of the mixture into balls. Place on the tray, leaving space between the balls. Moisten your fingers with a little water and press each ball to flatten it to 1 cm (¹/₂ in) thick.

Bake for 15 minutes, or until the edges of the biscuits are golden brown. Transfer to a wire rack to cool. If you are baking the biscuits in batches, make sure the baking tray is greased again each time. Store the cooled biscuits in an airtight container.

marbled meringues with raspberry cream

4 egg whites
220 g (1 cup) caster (superfine) sugar
2 teaspoons cornflour
1 teaspoon white vinegar
pink food colouring
300 ml (10^1/$_2$ fl oz) whipping cream
2 tablespoons icing (confectioners')
  sugar, sifted
1 teaspoon pure vanilla extract
150 g (5^1/$_2$ oz) fresh raspberries

Makes 20

Preheat the oven to 150°C (300°F/Gas 2). Cut out two pieces of baking paper large enough to line 2 baking trays. Draw ten 5 cm (2 in) circles on each piece of paper, then place on the trays, ink side down.

Put the egg whites in a clean, dry bowl. Using a hand-held electric beater beat the whites until soft peaks form. Gradually add the caster sugar, 1 tablespoon at a time, whisking well after each addition until the mixture is smooth and glossy. Sift in the cornflour, then fold in the vinegar. Sprinkle over a few drops of food colouring and fold through, marbling the mixture.

Pipe small mounds onto the baking paper, filling in the circle outlines. Put some food colouring into a bowl and dip a blunt knife into the colouring, then into the meringues, drawing swirls of colour through them.

Reduce the temperature to 140°C (275°F/ Gas 1) and bake for 1 hour. Turn off the oven and leave the meringues to cool.

Meanwhile, whisk together the cream, sugar and vanilla extract until soft peaks form. Put the raspberries in a bowl and gently crush with the end of a rolling pin. Fold into the cream. Sandwich the cooled meringues together with the raspberry cream. Serve within 2 hours of making.

tropical meringues

3 egg whites
175 g (3/4 cup) caster (superfine) sugar
50 g (generous 1/2 cup) desiccated
  coconut
1/4 teaspoon coconut essence
2 tablespoons milk
2 tablespoons caster (superfine) sugar
250 g (9 oz) mascarpone cheese
2 mangoes, peeled and thinly sliced
2 passionfruit, pulp only

Makes 6

Preheat the oven to 140°C (275°F/Gas 1). Grease and line two baking trays with baking paper. Put the egg whites in a dry bowl and whisk until soft peaks form. Add the sugar, 1 tablespoon at a time, until the mixture is stiff and glossy. Fold in the desiccated coconut and coconut essence.

Spoon 8 cm (3 in) mounds of the mixture onto the trays. Bake for 1 hour. Turn the oven off and leave for a further hour.

Add the milk and sugar to the mascarpone and whisk well. Dollop a little onto each meringue and top with the fruit.

mixed berry pavlova

4 egg whites, at room temperature
250 g (generous 1 cup) caster
   (superfine) sugar
500 g (2 1/4 cups) mascarpone cheese
300 g (10 1/2 oz) lemon curd
700 g (1 lb 9 oz) mixed berries, such as
   strawberries, blueberries and raspberries

Serves 8–10

Preheat the oven to 140°C (275°F/Gas 1).
Draw a 22 cm (9 in) circle on a piece of
baking paper. Put the paper on a lightly
greased baking tray, ink side down.

Put the egg whites in a large, clean, dry
glass or stainless steel bowl. Using a
hand-held or electric whisk, beat the egg
whites slowly until a frothy foam forms,
then increase the speed until the bubbles
have become small and evenly-sized.

When soft peaks have just formed, add
6 tablespoons of the sugar, 1 tablespoon
at a time, beating constantly. Add the
remaining sugar in a steady stream and
beat until the mixture is stiff and glossy
and all the sugar has dissolved. Don't over-
beat or the mixture will become grainy.

Pile the meringue high within the circle
marked on the baking paper and smooth
the top and sides with a palette knife,
making upward strokes around the edge.
This will help strengthen the sides of the
pavlova and give it a decorative finish.

Bake the pavlova for 1 1/2 hours then turn
off the oven and leave the pavlova to dry
out with the door slightly ajar.

When cold, remove the baking paper from
the bottom of the pavlova and transfer to
a serving plate. Whip the mascarpone and
lemon curd until well blended. Pile on top
of the pavlova and scatter over the mixed
berries. Serve at once.

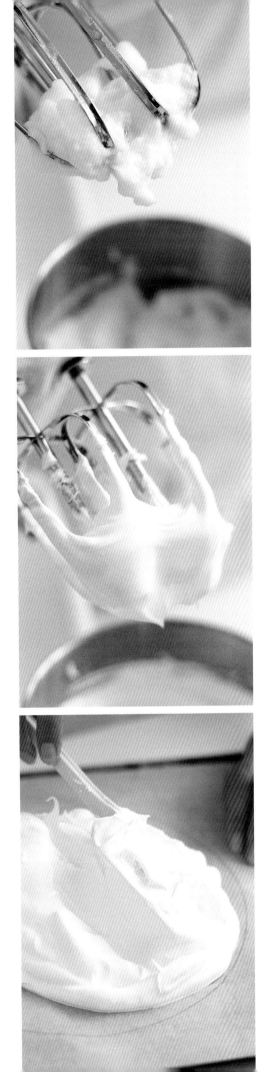

glossary

alcohol Egg-based dishes utilize a number of different alcohols—mostly in sweet ones but in savoury, as well. Some classic choices are sweet Marsala, a fortified wine from Sicily; mandorla, an almond-flavoured Marsala; and framboise eau de vie, a distilled brandy made from raspberries. Grand Marnier and Cointreau are also used.

baked custards This method of making custard has resulted in classic desserts such as crème brûlée and crème caramel. It is the proportion of milk versus cream and the mix of whole eggs or yolks that influence the outcomes. All are cooked without the interference of stirring, which allows the proteins to form a gel, resulting in a more solid texture. To help insulate it from high temperatures, the custard is often cooked in a water bath.

béarnaise sauce Named after the French province of Béarn, this is a thick, creamy pungent sauce made with butter, egg yolks, vinegar and tarragon. Serve with red meat, grilled (broiled) fish or vegetables.

blind bake This involves lining raw pastry with baking paper and weighting it with baking beads or rice. The pastry is then prebaked before any filling is added to ensure that the pastry is cooked through and will not become soggy when the filling is baked in it.

butter In egg cooking, two types are used: unsalted and salted. Unsalted is creamy and good for frying and cooking, particularly sweet dishes. Salted contains more milk solids and will burn more easily.

cheesecake There are countless versions of this cake, but it was the Americans who first made it famous. The New York version is made with cream cheese and cream or sour cream, and is the densest version of all. In Italy, they are usually made with sweetened ricotta cheese.

crème fraîche Translated from the French, crème fraîche means 'fresh cream', but it is actually cultured cream. It has a slightly nutty, sharp flavour. It is higher in butterfat than is sour cream, so it is creamier.

Frangelico This hazelnut-flavoured liqueur is used to flavour desserts such as biscuits and cheesecakes. It is thought to have been originally made by an Italian monk, who distilled wild hazelnuts and other natural flavourings. Today, hazelnuts are infused with alcohol and water, then the distilled liquid is flavoured with cocoa, coffee, vanilla, rhubarb and orange flowers.

hollandaise sauce This light French butter sauce is the ideal companion to poached fish and asparagus, as well as being the classic component of eggs benedict. Like mayonnaise, hollandaise is an emulsion made using egg yolks, but butter, rather than oil, is used, and the egg yolks are hot.

mayonnaise Strictly speaking, this contains only egg yolks, olive oil and vinegar or lemon juice, combined in an emulsion. The basic recipe can be varied in a number of ways, such as with mustard or garlic (to make aïoli). Commercial varieties have a 'softer' texture due to added water—add 1 teaspoon of water to every 300 ml (10¹/2 fl oz) home-made mayonnaise to achieve the same effect.

millefeuille Classically made with sheets of puff pastry rolled thin and then pricked to prevent the pastry 'puffing up' but retaining a very flaky texture. It is then separated by layers of cream, fruit or fruit purée, and served in slices.

mousse From the French term meaning 'froth' or 'foam'. A mousse is soft and airy and can be either sweet or savoury. Cold dessert mousses are usually based on a flavouring such as chocolate to which cream and eggs or egg whites are added.

pan bagnat This sandwich is a speciality of Nice, and was originally made by tossing pieces of stale bread into a niçoise salad to soak up the juices. Today, the process is reversed: the salad is tossed into the roll.

pancetta Italian cured belly pork, a similar cut to streaky bacon, but cured with salt and spices.

quiche A savoury dish originating in the Alsace Lorraine region of France. The classic quiche is quiche Lorraine, an open tart with a pastry base filled with eggs, cream and bacon and served hot or cold; variations today can include almost anything, for example onion, cheese, fish and herbs. Usually there is little meat.

soufflé A light and fluffy dish made with either a sweet or savoury base into which beaten egg whites are gently folded. A soufflé is held up by the beaten egg whites and hot air it contains. As it cooks, the air expands and pushes the mixture outwards, sometimes as much as doubling its height. It is important the egg whites are not too soft or the soufflé will not rise; nor too stiff or they will not mix into the base well and the cooked soufflé will contain blobs of white egg.

stirred custards These are often used as a sauce or as an ice cream base. They are not as solid as a baked custard because the stirring prevents the eggs from forming a gel. Instead, they should be soft and thickened but not set. Cooking in a double boiler or water bath will help moderate the temperature and allow for gradual cooking—a stirred custard should never come to the boil. Crème Anglaise is the classic custard sauce.

conversions

The recipes in this book were developed using a tablespoon measure of 20 ml. In some other countries the tablespoon is 15 ml. In most recipes, this difference will not be noticeable, but for recipes using baking powder, bicarbonate of soda and small amounts of flour and cornflour, we suggest that, if you are using the smaller tablespoon, you add an extra teaspoon for each tablespoon.

spoon measures

1/4 teaspoon	1.25 ml
1/2 teaspoon	2.5 ml
1 teaspoon	5 ml
1 tablespoon	20 ml

weight		liquid measures	
10 g	1/4 oz	15/20 ml	1/2 fl oz
15 g	1/2 oz	30 ml	1 fl oz
25/30 g	1 oz	60 ml	2 fl oz
35 g	11/4 oz	80 ml	21/2 fl oz
40 g	11/2 oz	100 ml	31/2 fl oz
55 g	2 oz	125 ml	4 fl oz
60 g	21/4 oz	150 ml	5 fl oz
70 g	21/2 oz	170 ml	51/2 fl oz
85 g	3 oz	185 ml	6 fl oz
90 g	31/4 oz	190 ml	61/2 fl oz
100 g	31/2 oz	200 ml	7 fl oz
115 g	4 oz	250 ml	9 fl oz
125 g	41/2 oz	290 ml	10 fl oz
140 g	5 oz	300 ml	101/2 fl oz
150 g	51/2 oz		
175 g	6 oz	400 ml	14 fl oz
200 g	7 oz	425 ml	15 fl oz
225 g	8 oz	455 ml	16 fl oz
250 g	9 oz	500 ml	17 fl oz
280 g	10 oz	570 ml	20 fl oz
300 g	101/2 oz	1 litre	35 fl oz
325 g	111/2 oz		
350 g	12 oz		
375 g	13 oz		
400 g	14 oz		
425 g	15 oz		
450 g	1 lb		

index

Published by Murdoch Books®, a division of Murdoch Magazines Pty Ltd.

Murdoch Books® Australia
GPO Box 1203
Sydney NSW 1045
Phone: + 61 (0) 2 4352 7000
Fax: + 61 (0) 2 4352 7026

Murdoch Books UK Limited
Ferry House
51–57 Lacy Road
Putney, London SW15 1PR
Phone: + 44 (0) 20 8355 1480
Fax: + 44 (0) 20 8355 1499

Creative Director, Designer: Marylouise Brammer
Editorial Director: Diana Hill
Editorial Project Manager: Margaret Malone
Production: Fiona Byrne
Food Editor: Katy Holder
Photographer: Ian Hofstetter
Stylist: Katy Holder
Food Preparation: Jo Glynn

Chief Executive: Juliet Rogers
Publisher: Kay Scarlett

Recipes developed and written by Sophie Braimbridge, Oi Cheepchaiissara, Jo Glynn,
Sarah Randell, Carol Selva Rajah, Maria Villegas, Priya Wickramasinghe and the Murdoch
Books Test Kitchen.

National Library of Australia Cataloguing-in-Publication Data
Egg: from benedict to brûlée.
Includes index. ISBN 1 74045 209 7.
1. Cookery (Eggs).
641.675

PRINTED IN SINGAPORE by Imago.
Printed 2003.
©Text, design and illustrations Murdoch Books® 2003.

The publisher thanks the following for their assistance: David Edmonds, Sydney; MUD
Australia; and Peppergreen Antiques, Berrima.

IMPORTANT: Those who might be at risk from the effects of salmonella food poisoning (the elderly, pregnant
women, young children and those suffering from immune deficiency diseases) should consult their GP with any
concerns about eating raw eggs.